A Lighthouse on the Top of a Hill in the Middle of Nowhere

How I Built a Lighthouse

By Allan McGuire

Aeterno Books
Newport, New Hampshire

ISBN 978-0-9997913-0-1

Published by
Aeterno Books
Newport, New Hampshire

www.ibuiltalighthouse.com

Dedicated to Pat McGuire, without whose pithy words of encouragement while struggling to decide if I should build this lighthouse or not, I might never have "… gotten of the pot."

Introduction

After retiring to the home we'd had built in a small town in western New Hampshire, I was looking for a challenging and rewarding project. I wanted to build a workshop, not the typical barn or garage style of building – something with character like our house which was built with the antique beams and wide boards of an 1835 barn. Around this time my wife and I took a trip to Nova Scotia where we saw our first pepper pot lighthouses.

A lifelong lighthouse buff, I began thinking maybe I could combine my love of lighthouses with my need for a workshop, and build my own pepper pot lighthouse. Made of wood, rather than masonry, these unique structures can be constructed using simple carpentry skills. Being square, rather than round, they provide more usable interior space. Best of all, their impressive shape offers the charm and allure only a lighthouse can provide. Everything seemed to line up.

I had no doubt that I possessed the skills to build a wood framed building, but I also knew a lighthouse would present some unusual challenges. Most pepper pots were constructed decades ago and their builders are long since gone. Without books, plans or old lighthouse builders available for how-to advice, the first question was how to design a lighthouse that would suit my needs using today's building techniques. Fortunately, at least seventeen genuine examples of pepper pot lighthouses still stand in Nova Scotia alone.

Once the design was done, there would be the hurdles of getting a building permit, finding and working with contractors, dealing with seasons and weather... each one can impact the project.

My greatest concern was my physical ability to do the work. Though I felt fit, I would be starting the actual building in my late sixties, a time when stamina and speed can be an issue. I'd done some building when I was a lot younger, but each year you get a tiny bit slower.

After a lot of discussions, consideration, and a final prod from my sister-in-law Pat, my wife Mary Lou and I decided to go ahead with the project: we would build a lighthouse in our back yard, and the sooner we started, the better.

Through this project we learned everything it takes to build a lighthouse. But more importantly, we learned about ourselves: our stamina, our ability to face and solve unforeseen problems and the satisfaction of meeting and working with some truly good people.

I kept a daily journal of what we felt and did during the first phase of building. Our level of urgency was highest during the race to get the building up and weather tight before the first snow flew. The finish work, though a challenging part of the project, was less time dependent.

After reading about our epic adventure, we hope someone will be inspired to build their own lighthouse. If so, I guarantee that your experiences will be both the same as ours and different... and quite interesting and enlightening.

Chapter 1

To succeed, however, in anything at all, one should go understandingly about his work.   Joshua Slocum

Why a Lighthouse?

A lot of people have asked "Why build a lighthouse?" Fair question, seeing we don't live within fifty miles of the ocean. I love lighthouses. Lighthouses have a unique lure, unlike any other form of building. As a boy growing up in Boston I was fascinated by the towering presence and unique light sequences of the various Boston Harbor lighthouses. Later in life, I saw many more lighthouses from a different perspective while sailing the coast of New England. I still can't pass up the opportunity to visit every lighthouse I see and, if allowed, make that long climb to the top.

At our last home I built a barn-shaped attached garage with a full basement workshop. Our current New Hampshire home had a garage, but no workshop. I really needed space to house my collection of tools and to work on "old guy" projects.

At first we weren't sure what style of building we'd build. A barn or garage is simple, but not very exciting. We looked at designs such as carriage houses. We even thought of copying the small colonial mill, with a stone first story and framed second story, located in a nearby town. Nothing felt exactly right. But, we knew if we were going to all the effort and expense of building our own structure, we wanted one with character.

I hadn't thought of a lighthouse as an option. Most lighthouses are circular towers made of masonry or cast iron and almost entirely consumed by internal staircases. I had visited a couple that were square house-like structures with a tower on top. The first floor would be ideal for a workshop, but the tower would be too small to be useful, considering the effort required to build it.

We were on a trip to Nova Scotia to research my wife Mary Lou's genealogy when we discovered the charm and beauty of the Canadian pepper pot lighthouses. The first one we saw was outside the Welcome Center at the entry to Nova Scotia from New Brunswick. Our interest piqued, we picked up information on the Lighthouse Route, a tour guide publication featuring many lighthouses.

The first pepper pot we visited is on the lawn of the Age of Sail Heritage Museum in Port Greville, Nova Scotia. It had originally served as the Port Greville Harbor light before being moved to its current site. Passing through its doorway, I got a comfortable feeling, similar to being in an old log cabin. It's tilted walls and rugged framing gave an older, more homey sense than you'd get from a stick-frame house or garage. Its design captured my imagination, and I began thinking there just might be a pepper pot lighthouse in our future.

Over the next winter I researched more of these unique buildings on the Internet. The best source of information was the Nova Scotia Lighthouse Preservation Society website. It provided a wealth of information on seventeen pepper pot style lighthouses that still exist in Nova Scotia, including their history, dimensions and locations.

We planned another trip north the following summer, this time to take our own lighthouse tour. Our stops were the lighthouses closest in size to what I might be able build myself. We included a stop at Brier Island. Their octagonal lighthouse wasn't what I was thinking of building, but a visit to the boyhood home of Joshua Slocum couldn't help but provide inspiration for my own single-handed project.

We narrowed our options to four-sided lighthouses, believing the six or eight sided buildings too difficult to build. We soon discovered that other than having tapered walls, no two pepper pots are the same. It seems each builder modified a basic design to meet specific local needs, budget or artistic taste.

Examples of Lighthouse Designs

Most of these lighthouses have a deck twenty feet or more above the ground. On some the deck is narrow, on others wider decks overhang the side walls, often with fascia boards to create a graceful curved effect from wall to deck bottom.

Windows vary from tiny, to large, to none at all. The window dormers have either peaked or flat shed roofs.

The lamp room, or what some call the lantern room, is the glassed-in area housing the light. These structures vary greatly in size and shape. Some have sloped sides, carrying the lines of the walls all the way to the roof. Others are four or six sided with perpendicular walls. Lamp room heights range from just a few feet, with hatch access to the deck, to being high enough to stand in with a door to the outside deck.

Some lighthouses sit on foundations, but pilings are common. Though footprint sizes vary, the slope of their walls always seems proportionate to their height.

Armed with a lot of pictures and a ton of features in mind, I returned home, fired up to start designing. I felt that by drawing the design myself I'd get a true grasp on what would actually be involved before making the final commitment to take on such a big project: which features to include, how much work it would take and, most importantly, could I actually build it?

On the plus column I had some building experience. I'd designed and built a three story building with a workshop, two garage bays and a loft. I'd also helped friends with home building and additions. I have project management experience, some skill in mechanical drawing and can read blue prints.

On the maybe column, I was almost sixty-seven years old. I was in pretty good shape, but my knees and back weren't as forgiving as they used to be, and I was close to having shoulder surgery.

On the negative column, if we started building and for some reason couldn't finish, my wife or I might have difficulty finding anyone capable – or willing – to finish such an odd building.

One thing for sure, if we were going to take on a project this involved, we'd best start sooner rather than later.

I contacted the Canadian Coast Guard, who has jurisdiction over the lighthouses, to see if there were any design guidelines or plans in their archives. The couple of old plans they sent me were too sketchy be of any practical use. Without existing plans, I'd have to do what they probably did in the old days: design my lighthouse from scratch to suit specific needs.

The final issue of the design process would be approval. Having designed my own non-typical structure, would the town allow me to build it? This could be a gamble. What if I designed the entire structure, only to find I couldn't get a building permit?

I decided to take a risk and go ahead with the design. All I had to lose at this point was time. In our part of New Hampshire if you don't ski, snowshoe or have a heated workshop, you have lots of free time over the long winter. My new hobby on those cold winter days would be to design a lighthouse.

Chapter 2

Preliminary Design

One advantage of not using an existing design was the freedom to create whatever I wanted. The size of the building, number of windows, shape of the deck and lamp room were my variables. However, I knew it was important to keep in mind that every feature costs time, materials and labor.

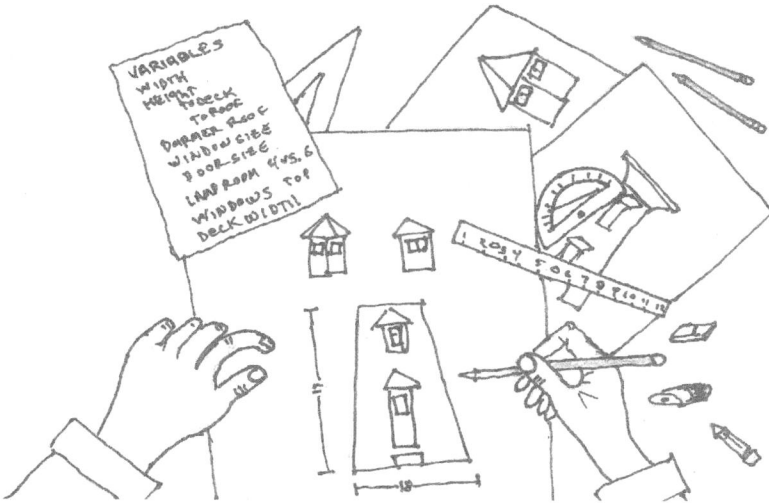

I began with the foundation. To me, basements are dark, musty spaces that fill themselves with junk you never use. I built a basement workshop once, but never felt comfortable working in it. My lighthouse would not have a basement. It would either sit on posts with a wooden first floor, or have poured frost walls with a cement slab floor.

Posts would be more economical. I could dig the holes and pour the posts myself using Sonotubes. But posts create the problems of a crawl space. Animals love living in crawl spaces, and cold winter winds can howl through below the floor. Since we lived near the very top of an over 1300' hill, subject to high winds from the valley below, a solid foundation would be safest. However, it would also be harder to build and more expensive. In this area, walls have to be on footings that go down at least four feet to compensate for frost. Even so, the more costly poured foundation was the way we decided to go.

Next, I listed the features I wanted to incorporate in the structure. My basic goal for the building was for it to really look like a pepper pot lighthouse, not just a box with tilted walls. Therefore height, width and the slant of the walls had to be in the proper proportion. I needed a workshop on the first floor, and a usable room on the second floor, both with high ceilings. I wanted a staircase to the second floor, but felt a ladder to the lamp room would be okay. I also wanted standing room in the lamp room, a door rather than a hatch out to the deck, and enough room to walk around on the outside deck. The lamp room would need a reasonably pitched roof, considering our snowfall. And finally, the total building height couldn't exceed 35 feet, to comply with the local building code.

After averaging out the tapering, or slopes, of the pepper pots I'd seen, walls standing at an angle of 79°, or 11° shy of perpendicular, appeared to capture the correct visual effect. This became my "magic angle," the one that wound up on the top, bottom, end or beveled edge of nearly every piece of wood in the first two stories.

I figured an 18′ square first floor would offer adequate space for a workshop, assuming most of it wasn't consumed by stairs or broken up by posts. The height of the first and second floor ceilings should be at least 8′ to avoid feeling cramped by the inward sloping walls. But the higher the ceilings, the more stairs are required and the smaller the above floor space.

I love the look of a lighthouse with decks that project beyond the tops of the walls, but I had a lot to consider before including them in my design. Often a curved fascia runs from the bottom of the outer edge of the overhang to a point one or more feet down the wall above the highest dormer roof. The exact spot depends on how far the deck overhangs.

The fascia, window size, type of dormer roof, story heights, deck size, lamp room height and lamp room roof all combine to determine the overall height of the building.

We preferred good sized windows set in peaked roof dormers. This in itself adds to the second story height. Adding space for a curved fascia makes the second story even taller. Taking into consideration the inward slope of the wall, the taller the second story gets, the more deck overhang. A wider overhang is more complicated to frame and increases the exposure to snow loading. Also, the taller the second story, the steeper the ladder to the lamp room.

I played around with all the variables, and came to the conclusion that to incorporate the curved fascias I'd need to make the foundation bigger and the lighthouse taller. I could do this and still be under the maximum height of 35 feet, but the additional work and construction cost was hard to justify in my mind. It was a tough decision, but I traded off overhanging decks for simplicity and cost.

After figuring out how everything should look, I was ready to begin my detailed design. I began by drawing an 18' wide foundation and then ran corner lines up at 11° off perpendicular. I stopped at the point where the deck was 12' wide.

Next I drew two lamp room designs, one with four sides and the other with six. Both had a 3' high roof adequately sloped to handle snow and a full size door leading to the deck. With 8' walls to accommodate the door, the lamp room was about 11' tall.

Matching each lamp room design with the design of the main structure, showed that the 12' square deck with minimal overhang provided enough space to walk around the outside of the lamp room.

Of the two designs, the six sided lamp room would be more work to build, but this time… looks won.

The first two floors came out to be a total of 22' high, including above ground foundation. The overall building height is 32 feet.

Everything seemed to naturally fit. Satisfied with my rough design, it was time to add some detail.

Initial Concept

Chapter 3
Adding Details

At this point I thought of switching to a CAD package. Unable to find one that lent itself to slanted wall construction, I continued with graph paper and pencil. This just felt right. Drawing, erasing and redrawing would help me understand and tune how all the components fit together.

There are several structural differences in a building with slanted walls. Intuitively, walls tilted inward toward the center should be sturdier than perpendicular walls. When horizontal wind pressure is applied each wall works against the opposite wall, which is canted against the force. One Nova Scotia pepper pot has faced the ravages of ocean storms and hurricanes since 1875, and is still standing.

The effect of pressure from the top, such as the weight of the building and its contents, is not so obvious. Downward pressure wants to push the bottoms of the canted walls apart. This can be counteracted by bolting the floors to each other and the sills to the foundation.

From the pepper pots I'd visited, the preferred wall studs appeared to be rough cut 2×8's on 16" or wider centers. I decided to use 2×8's on 16" centers in my design. This is way above code for stick frame buildings. An added advantage of the bigger studs is their wider header and footer plates, which provide more corner overlap and area for seating the floor joists for the second floor and the deck. It turned out that with 2×8 studs cut at the magic 11°angle, the top and bottom plates had to be 2×10's.

Rather than common dimensional lumber for the floor joists, I went with engineered wooden joists or I-Joists. Similar in form to a steel I-beam, I-Joists support greater weight than common lumber and do not sag or spring. They could easily span the top of the first floor without the need for supporting posts and give added strength beneath the deck and lamp room structure. I went with the 16" on center for the I-Joists as well. According to specs, I could have gone wider, but a few extra joists would give me added confidence and have minimal impact on the overall cost.

Each door and window means more work, cost and time. To get the natural light and views that were important to us, both floors needed at least two windows. The first floor main entry door, on the east side, would have a window and the south facing wall would have a full window. Placing the second floor windows above the main door and in the opposing west wall gives balance to the design and offers cross ventilation. The windows and doors would be set in tall, shallow dormers to account for the slant of the wall. I designed the dormers with peaked roofs. Although harder to construct than shed roofs, their better look is worth the effort.

Next, the staircases. Staircases are always a challenge. The lighthouses we had visited used stair ladders between floors because they take up far less floor space than a traditional staircase. Unless going to a loft – in our case the lamp room – they aren't code compliant. A traditionally framed, code compliant staircase would eat up too much floor space, and the higher the ceiling, the more space consumed. But a spiral staircase footprint is independent to its height. The disadvantages of a spiral staircase are higher cost, less comfort to climb, and less maneuvering space when carrying large items. All this in mind, we decided on a spiral staircase from the first to the second floor.

A stair ladder would be fine between the second floor to the lamp room. Cheaper and more simple to build, it would consume less of the smaller second floor space. A close-able hatch above the ladder makes the entire limited lamp room floor space usable.

My basic design was done. I had created a separate plan for each side wall, each floor, the lamp room walls, the dormers, the roof, the frost walls and drawn a loci plan showing the location of the building on the lot. Now, the big question, would the town let me build it?

Chapter 4

Gaining Approval

Even though we live in a rural area, our town has zoning, approval processes, and requires inspections for each stage of the building. I had researched wood framing, but hadn't found any rules or guidelines for buildings with slanted walls. With detailed plans, including every stud and joist from the foundation up to the roof, I was sure my design far exceeded building codes. But those codes were really intended for perpendicular walls.

I was worried that all the time I spent planning and designing would be for naught if my non-standard, slant sided building was rejected by the town planning office. I was also worried that I might be dismissed as some kind of a nut with a crazy plan to build a lighthouse in the middle of the woods.

It was time to find out. I made copies of my twenty-plus pages of hand-drawn prints, and set up a meeting with the building inspector to review what I called my "workshop." Assuming approval, our June 6th meeting would be the formal start of the building phase of the project.

I opened our meeting by telling him where I lived and that I was planning to build a

My Pile of Plans

workshop. Then I handed him a set of my plans. The cover sheet clearly showed a lighthouse. His response was silence, accompanied by patient head nodding. The silence was deafening. I hurriedly started pitching my rationale of why I wanted my workshop to look like a lighthouse. Then, to head off possible objections to the slanted walls, I went into the sizes of the studs, my theory of slanted walls and how sturdy the building would actually be. After hearing me out, he had several questions, but didn't seem overly concerned with my sanity or the non-standard aspects of the design.

Our discussion moved to the ultimate use of the building. He pointed out something that I did not know. Our town zoning allowed for the addition of mother-in-law apartments. Unlike in some other towns, the apartment could be detached from the main dwelling. If I made some modification to comply with building codes for a dwelling, in the future my lighthouse could be living space. I envisioned one of those tiny houses they show on television. I had no plan to live in the lighthouse, but built properly, it could add far more future value to the property than a mere workshop.

The changes to make it dwelling compliant didn't seem to significantly alter the cost or time to build. I'd have to meet insulation standards, but I was going to insulate it for winter use anyway. I'd have to include smoke and monoxide detectors, and change the size of at least one window. Code required a double hung window large enough for a fireman to enter with an air bottle on his back. Roughed-in pipes for a bathroom and kitchen could be added at minimal cost before the slab was poured.

The inspector closed, adding that he was not familiar with this style of building and wanted an architect to review my design. Familiar with the elevation and exposure to high winds on our lot, he recommended an assessment of the strength of the slanted walls and their anchoring to the foundation. I agreed, confident this would not be a problem. I'd just cleared the first hurdle in what would turn out to be a long race.

I needed to briefly return to design mode. The first step to enlarge the second story window meant making the dormer larger. I couldn't see having one window bigger than the others, so all three walls with windows had to be laid out again to accommodate larger dormers. I also needed to draw up a rough plumbing design. That would involve changes to the slab and foundation plans.

On paper, design changes are simple to make, but each change usually adds to the project time and cost. One of my goals from the outset was to avoid the deadly phenomenon of project creep, in which one change leads to another and the end date and budget continually go out and up.

I became fascinated by the idea of not only building a lighthouse/workshop, but also making it a tiny house. There was some solace in knowing that if I drove Mary Lou crazy while building the thing, I'd have a new place to live. Maybe some day I'd rent it out like an Airbnb. After all, who wouldn't like to spend a night in a lighthouse, especially the highest lighthouse in New Hampshire?

I knew an architect in town. I called and explained what I was doing, and asked if she'd review my design. She and her partner agreed to stop by the next week to look over my plans. That would give me enough time to make the changes.

When it comes to projects, my biggest flaw is optimism. Excluding things like neurosurgery, in my mind, given access to the right information, I can do anything. I have the same optimism when it comes to managing my time. If someone else is doing the work, my estimates are usually quite accurate. If I'm doing the work myself, my time estimates are best-case to far better.

I may be an optimist, but not a fool. It was now part way through June. It was already iffy to get the whole project completed in one season. From this day forward, a guy my age with his completely inexperienced wife as his main helper, would really have to manage the time. It would be a push. We had four to five months, depending on weather, to at least get the building up and weather tight before the first snow. For some parts of the project, such as foundation work, I'd have to rely on contractors... who I had yet to find.

Chapter 5

Digging Down

A lighthouse is an impressive building. It is important that it fits with adjoining structures and doesn't overpower them.

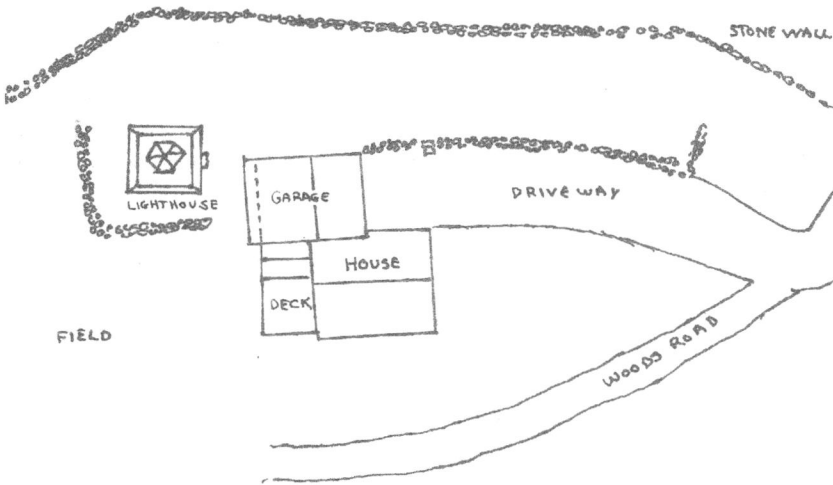

Loci Plan

On June 7th I began finalizing the exact spot for the foundation. Our lot is big, nearly eleven acres, but hilly. The house and garage are an L-shaped configuration. We'd positioned the house at nearly the highest elevation on the lot for the best view. The corner of the garage is within fifty feet of the lot line. Behind the garage is a sloping cleared area of about half an acre with a few trees along the highest part. The low end of the clearing has the underground septic system that cannot be built on. The remaining cleared area looked to have plenty of space for an 18×18' structure. The question was exactly where to put it.

I wanted my lighthouse to command the greatest view, but was concerned that in the wrong place it would look like a Godzilla looming up behind the garage, decreasing rather than increasing the property value.

Looking at an empty field, it is hard to visualize how much space a building will take. I folded and duct taped a couple of old tarps into a large 18×18' square, the footprint of my lighthouse. I dragged the tarp around the yard, looking for the best site for the building, and found that midway between the septic and the lot line appeared to be ideal. This gave up a few vertical feet of view, but was far beyond the required setback from the lot line in the building code. The lighthouse would also not be visible from the front of the house.

Before a building can go up, you need to dig down. Whatever was lurking below the surface of the ground would determine how difficult it would be to dig the foundation hole.

On June 8th I made my first project purchase other than graph paper: a bundle of wooden stakes. I put stakes three feet beyond the edges of the tarp. This included enough space to pour the footings and set the forms for the walls. Footings must be four feet deep to compensate for the frost. The exception to this rule is when they sit on solid ledge.

When God created the earth he must have dumped the extra rocks in western New Hampshire. Every spring the frost pops stones, ranging from the size of potatoes to basketballs, out of the soil. The small ones are no problem. The big ones and ledges can make things difficult.

In the past, holes dug in other areas on the lot uncovered a variety of subsoil from sand, to clay with rocks, to solid ledge. I suspected the spot I'd chosen would have sand or clay and loose rock. If sand, I'd be in luck. Maybe I'd rent a mini-excavator and get the foundation hole dug while waiting on the architectural review. But if big rocks were down there, a mini excavator couldn't handle them. I needed to know what I was dealing with.

I tried probing around the area to be dug with a steel rod. That didn't work. My probe never got down more than a couple of feet, and I couldn't tell if I was hitting medium rocks, big rocks or solid ledge. I had to dig some test holes.

Armed with pick and shovel, I began digging a test trench. The going was slow and tough. The subsoil turned out to be hard clay loaded with rocks. Exhausted, I gave up at the end of the day. All I had to show for my effort was a 6×2, 3' deep hole, a pile of clay and lots of rocks. Digging by hand would take forever.

The next morning I went to see about renting a mini-excavator, at least for a day. I was struck with sticker shock. Mini-excavators rent for $450 a day or $1050 a week plus delivery. After a lengthy discussion, the rental guy, who at the time was building his own house, suggested that rather than rent a machine I should think about hiring a dirt guy. He highly recommended the guy who dug his foundation hole. This guy was "Really fast and a magician with an excavator."

I returned home with a new problem to fret over. If a mini-excavator was $450 per day, what would a full size excavator with an operator cost? It could be much more expensive and, even worse, take a lot of time to find a guy and get on his schedule. I walked out to my job site to ponder the situation.

Surprise! It hadn't rained, but overnight my little trench somehow wound up with two feet of standing water. How the water table near the top of a huge hill could be so shallow was beyond me. The only reason I could guess was an underground spring. Obviously, I'd have to move the lighthouse. Uphill looked like the best alternative. The higher the elevation the better the view. It would also make the lighthouse visible from the driveway in front of the garage. And the higher I went up the hill, the closer I got to the solid ledge exposed just beyond the back corner of the garage. The next day became a re-planning day. I was spending more time re-planning than working.

It is good to know exactly what you want, when you need it, and how much you are willing to pay before meeting with a contractor. When both parties understand the job, it's much easier to get a clear price and schedule. I was itching to call the dirt guy, but wasn't exactly sure where the hole would be. With the site moving up hill, I was also fretting about the height of the lighthouse versus the garage.

Using graph paper, I made a scale profile model of the house and garage. I also made a scale model of the lighthouse. With the models stapled to wooden blocks, I was able to move the lighthouse around behind the garage, varying the height as it moved uphill. Placing my head at the level of the driveway, I got a perspective of what the lighthouse would look like to someone standing in front of the garage. Even after shifting the lighthouse the equivalent of about thirty feet up the hill, all that could be seen from the driveway was the lamp room. It looked to be centered behind the garage roof. Now I knew exactly where I wanted the lighthouse to sit.

The new site extended beyond the cleared area, and was partially covered by scrub trees, brush and a few old stumps. I spent the next couple of days clearing brush.

On the 16th I did a final re-staking of the outer boundaries for the foundation hole. Ten days had passed since getting approval and I was just now ready to contact the dirt guy.

Dealing with contractors can be a tremendous hassle. Given they are available and interested in doing a job, after negotiating to get to a reasonable price, you have no guarantee they will come in on bid or on time. It's a real crap shoot. In our area most contractors prefer running a tab. They figure in so much per hour and guess on the number of hours. In some cases you can't fault this. They don't know what's under the dirt either. I prefer doing things myself, but some jobs I can't do, especially since I don't own an excavator.

I called Mark, the dirt guy. It was about four o'clock in the afternoon. Mark said that he was working on a job in the area and could swing by in a couple of hours to look at the job. He had a free day this week to do the digging. Alarms went off in my head. If he was so good, why was he instantly available?

Mark showed up two hours later, as promised. We went behind the garage to the site with stakes in place. I discovered the unplanned, sort of natural ritual of toe-kicking the soil that occurred with every contractor or inspector who visited the site.

I pointed out the nearby exposed ledge, and asked about getting the machine onto the site. The only apparent path was a road I'd cut through the woods. It ran from about half way up my driveway to the cleared area behind the garage. It would require navigating the excavator below a huge tilted birch tree and then up the hill between the septic field and the house. We walked that path.

Mark, a can-do guy, was sure that getting the machine in would be no problem. "You know you're going to probably hit ledge under there, don't you?" I agreed. "Okay, but some of the stone I pull out might be pretty big pieces that will be hard to get out of here." That was not an issue. We agreed he'd take any stones that came out of the hole and line them up to make the start of a wall on the downhill slope, in effect creating the basis of an island of flat land around the lighthouse.

We closed with an agreement on where he'd pile the dirt from the hole. Mark promised to return in two days with his machine. Amazingly, the estimate of one day digging, assuming no problems, plus delivering the machine, was less than the cost of the mini-excavator for the week.

The next day the architect and her partner stopped by the site. I showed them the plans and explained the building inspector's concerns. They took a set of plans and promised to look them over and get back to me soon. I stressed that time was of the essence. I'd keep moving forward on the foundation, because nothing they came up with would affect that.

I double-checked my stakes and again updated my loci plan. I also called the forms guy Mark had recommended, and left a voicemail to set up a meeting to discuss the cement work.

Early on the morning of June 18th I awoke to a rumbling noise and a trembling house. Ledge transmits the shock of heavy equipment crawling by to anything sitting on the same underlying ledge. I hurried to the site. It was time to play supervisor: watch someone else work.

Excavators are awesome machines. It took less than half an hour for the excavator to pop out all the old stumps and throw them down the hill into my brush pile. My procrastination in pulling them out myself when I'd cut down the trees had paid off.

Then the serious digging began. Stone after chunk of loose ledge came out of the hole. Mark piled the bigger pieces, one measuring about 8×2×3', across the slope. He pulled loose dirt for future back fill behind them. The bucket screeched and scraped as it clawed against and uncovered permanently attached ledge. The resulting hole was not the cube shaped flat bottomed hole of my original foundation plan. The solid ledge was a little over a foot below the surface on the top side, and sloped down to about a five foot depth on the downhill side.

Mark suggested that the only way to make a traditional foundation hole would be to blast out the ledge, but common practice was to leave the ledge in place and pin the footings to it. Pinning would avoid dynamiting and rubble removal. It would save on concrete, but would be harder to form. Since I was planning on no basement, but just filling below the slab with sand, pinning was the way to go.

Mark had lived up to his reputation. He was a magician with an excavator, coming in on time, one day, and on budget. Things were looking good. Before leaving, he asked how I planned to fill around the outside and below the slab. I wasn't sure. I'd originally planned to use the dirt that came out of the hole as back fill, but almost none came out of the hole. Most of what he'd dug out was the stone that was now the beginnings of a wall.

I would need tons of sand for back fill. The excavator had been able to crawl in through the woods road, but dump trucks full of sand couldn't use the same route. Getting the sand from where a truck could dump it, hundreds of feet to the site, would be the challenge. Mark didn't sound interested in that job, but did say that he would sell and deliver the sand.

Another thing to fret over. But it didn't have to be solved until after the footings and walls were poured, and I didn't even have a cement guy yet. So far, building my wooden lighthouse was an exercise in planning and digging. With moving sand, filling in holes and getting a foundation and slab poured, would I ever get to the actual framing part?

The Hole

23

Chapter 6

More Planning

I spent the next morning updating the plan for the foundation to reflect the ledge, and that the footings would be pinned to it. Then I was off to the building inspector. Happily, ledge pinning was not an issue. I also found out that, if I did it to code, I could do my own electrical wiring and rough plumbing. New Hampshire stands by its "Live Free or Die" motto. I could save some money by doing it myself, but now had to add figuring out how to do the plumbing design to my list of things to fret over.

I went home, scraped the loose dirt from the ledge, and spray-painted the location of the foundation corners for future reference by the cement guy.

That afternoon the architect called to tell me she was not the right kind of architect for my job. I needed an architect who does structural engineering. She suggested a few names and agreed to return her set of the plans. Hopefully I'd still have time to get the review done without having to delay the actual build.

The next day my approved insulation plan was returned by the State. In rural areas the town doesn't approve or inspect insulation, approval is the responsibility of the State. Inspection can be done by the installer. No matter, if the building is ever to be a dwelling it, including the foundation, must be insulated to code.

I began calling my leads for a structural architect. I've worked with engineers for years, but after living for a while in one of the lowest tech parts of the country, I had forgotten how weird communicating with them can be.

The first architect let me spend over fifteen minutes explaining what I was doing and what I needed before telling me, in a convoluted way, that he didn't want the job. Even though he worked out of his home, he didn't do jobs that small. Even if he did take jobs that small, he couldn't because he was too busy. Maybe he could do the job if he found some time. Just in case, I should send him a detailed set of plans and an email description of everything I needed in case he could help. Sure! A good idea: avoid anyone who starts off by telling you he doesn't want the job.

The next architect was more direct. He understood exactly what I needed and thought it would be interesting. But he was very busy and couldn't take on anything new for months. If I couldn't find someone he might be able to do the job next winter. I was down to one name. If he couldn't do the job, the delay could push the project into next year and I would be left with a hole big enough to bury an elephant behind my garage and the summer off.

Fortunately the third try was the charm. He understood exactly what I wanted and when I needed it. If I sent him a full set of plans and a letter with the specifics, he'd squeeze the job in. We agreed on a price for him to analyze the stresses on the building and provide a written report including his calculations and a list of recommended design changes. First thing the next morning my letter and plans were in the mail, and I was off to meet with the building supply center.

Another good idea: when beginning a building project, set up a relationship with a reputable lumberyard. In our town we are lucky to have one of the best in the area. I had my first meeting at LaValley Building Supply and Todd, my account rep. I got to explain to yet another stranger that I had this plan to build a lighthouse. I must have been getting good at it. He acted as if it was a normal thing to do. Maybe I was just being paranoid and people didn't think I was nuts, but isn't being paranoid being nuts? I set up a charge account. Monthly billing is very convenient.

An additional benefit of working with a large lumberyard is they know every tradesman in the area. The contact Mark had given me for a concrete guy hadn't answered my calls. I got a few new leads from Todd.

Chapter 7

Filling the Hole

The first cement guy I reached was Andy. He agreed to look at the job the next day. Some contractors never call back while others are readily available. Often a contractor gets delayed starting a job by the contractor before him not finishing on time. The smarter ones use small jobs to fill these gaps in their schedules. To me, my lighthouse was a mega project. To most contractors, the jobs I needed done were small.

That evening I calculated how much concrete it should take to pour the footings, walls and slab. I found a cost range on the internet and felt comfortable that I knew what would be a reasonable price. I knew a concrete truck couldn't make it onto the site, but it could pull up close to the front of the garage, and the path to the site was just four feet above the driveway. They could pour the concrete into wheelbarrows and push it the seventy feet or so to the far end of the footing. I figured this would increase the labor cost and added in a fudge factor to my estimate.

Andy showed up as promised. We went out to the site and kicked some dirt. I showed him my plans. He took some of his own measurements and told me that he'd have to build the footing forms by hand. They would be stepped in several places to compensate for the slope of the ledge, providing flat bases for the foundation forms. Then he'd drill into the granite and set the pins. After the footings were poured, conventional forms would be set up on the stepped footings and the walls would get poured. After they stripped the forms I would need to do the back filling, coating, insulating, inside filling and compacting. I'd then call to let him know that the inside was ready and he'd return and pour the slab. Simple enough!

He asked how I had planned to get the concrete onto the site. I told him my wheelbarrow idea and got a quick and solid "Nope." The concrete had to be pumped. A pumper truck would extend its boom over the garage and the boom would swing from form to form. The pumper cost is $750 per visit, one for the footings and another for the walls. He agreed to consider using wheelbarrows for the slab since it would only take a couple of yards of material. A trip to his pickup in the driveway and a few minutes on a calculator resulted in an estimate of about $6500. I winced. My estimate was $4500, but it hadn't figured in enough for building the custom footing forms or $1500 for renting the pumpers. I agreed to the deal and he agreed to start in about a week, depending on other jobs finishing on time and the weather, but for sure close to that. I stressed how time was of the essence. He nodded and smiled.

It was now over three weeks into June. I had a hole dug, a concrete guy lined up, and time before he would start. There were plenty of jobs to fill that time. I decided to figure out how to do the rough plumbing so that I could get the plans approved and the pipe laid before the slab got poured.

My plumbing experience was limited to soldering pipes and attaching fixtures. I got two books on plumbing from the library. After researching shower and toilet dimensions on the web, I drew up my version of a plumbing design and added it to the slab plan. I carefully figured how deep the drain exit from the foundation needed to be to meet the required slope going down the hill to the existing septic tank. The book stressed that proper pipe slope is a big deal.

Though what I'd laid out for the sub-floor drains looked right according to the book, I wasn't all that confident with my first plumbing design. If I had screwed it up, down the road it would take a jack hammer to chop it out of the slab.

Fretting about the plumbing I might never use felt nonproductive. I needed to talk to a real plumber. I took my plans to the guy who had plumbed our house. He scanned my design and handed it back saying it was simpler than that. If I called him once the sand was in the foundation he'd send a guy out to rough it in. His estimate of about $400, including materials, seemed like a good deal.

Physically, I took the next day off. Mentally, it was impossible to shut down even when I wasn't working.

The next day I called Andy to check on his schedule. He might begin in two days, depending on weather. That night I lay in bed listening to torrential rains and envisioning the hole filling with water. The next morning I slogged through fresh mud to the site. The half-full hole looked like a muddy swimming pool. I needed to dig a drainage ditch. The temperature was in the high eighties with saturating humidity. I spent the whole morning digging and sweating through two shirts. I gave up in exhaustion several feet before reaching the hole. Maybe I was getting a bit too old for pick and shovel work. That night it rained again. The pool got deeper. No chance of getting custom footing forms built in a hole full of water. If the forms guys showed up on time, they'd reschedule. I couldn't afford that. The next morning, after a couple of two hour shifts in the muggy heat with help from Mary Lou, we busted through. Hundreds of gallons of water gushed through our little canal and down the hill.

On July 1st the forms guys showed up to check out the site. Thankfully, it was nearly dry. I spent the rest of the day running a circuit from the house electrical panel through the garage to under the overhang of the back garage roof. This provided power for their drill as well as my air compressor and other power tools, on the remote chance I might ever get to frame the building.

Less than twelve hours after I had hooked up the electricity, Andy's guys were drilling holes for the pins. As they built the footing forms I put together PVC pipes to go through the wall for attaching conduits. There were three on the side nearest the garage. One for a future water feed from the well, another for the underground power feed and the third for extraneous wires such as coax and networking from the house. A paint can in the downhill wall would provide an opening for the soil pipe exit to the septic field. I updated the final pipe positions on my foundation plan.

Work ceased on the foundation from the 4th through the 7th because of the Fourth of July weekend. Apparently nobody pours cement on long holiday weekends, and even if they wanted to, nobody sells or pumps it. Andy's guys assured me that the forms, which were still only partly done, would get finished the morning before the cement truck and pumper showed up.

Pumping Concrete

Pouring the Footing

Just before noon on July 8th, they drove the final nails into the footing forms as the pumper truck pulled in. Shortly after, the massive machine was in position with its hydraulic outriggers extended. Then the cement truck arrived. The boom swung up and over the garage and cement plopped its way out and into the forms. Six yards of concrete later, the footings were poured. Everyone disappeared as quickly as they appeared, leaving me alone to dig a trench for the underground conduit from the rear of the garage over to the foundation hole. I didn't hit rocks or ledge and, despite the heat, the digging was the easiest I'd encountered to date.

On the morning of the 9th they stripped the forms. The footings looked large enough to support a hotel... truly impressive, but soon to be buried. The footing at the top of the hill was higher than I'd planned. I needed to adjust the plan to correctly reflect the ground clearance... back to the drawing board.

Later in the day the cement guys returned and put up the wall forms. I showed them where all the through holes would be, gave them the fittings I'd made, and finalized where the anchor bolts should go. I'd spaced the anchors closer together and made them longer than required in anticipation that the architect would come back with more demanding than standard recommendations. I double-checked to make sure no bolt lined up exactly with a stud or the doorway.

Wednesday morning the building inspector dropped by and approved the footings. After a round of heavy showers, the pumper reappeared. The cement trucks followed and several more tons of concrete went over the garage into the wall forms. Just as they were finishing, the skies opened up again. I covered the walls with tarps and headed out to buy conduit. Returning with the conduit, I noticed something odd. While I was gone either the cement truck driver or, more likely, the pumper driver, had decided to clean his equipment. He'd dumped over a yard of excess concrete two feet off the side of my driveway. I don't know what he was thinking, but a giant concrete lump wasn't what I wanted to see every time I drove up the driveway for the rest of my life. Fortunately, the rain had stopped and the pile was still somewhat soft. I grabbed a hoe and spent the rest of the day dragging concrete down a slope into the woods. Why he couldn't have asked where to dump it, beats me. Ironically, the slogan painted on the side of the pumper was "Pump It Don't Dump It." It started to rain again just as I finished. The thrill of getting the foundation poured had been replaced by complete exhaustion.

On July 17th they stripped the forms. The walls looked great.

The Foundation

Chapter 8

Getting to the Slab

The foundation walls were up, but there was still a ton of work to do before the slab could be poured. First, the outside of the foundation needed to be sealed with asphalt foundation coating. The theory being, a sealed foundation doesn't absorb water and dampness. I also had to run the three conduits for wiring and water and connect them to the fittings going through the foundation. Then I had to insulate the inside of the foundation before back filling. I don't get the theory behind insulating a foundation that was going to be filled with sand, but the instructions from the State of New Hampshire said do it, so I did it.

It was really hot again, but at least it wasn't raining. I cleaned out my conduit trench and glued the conduits to the thru-foundation fittings and up the inner wall to beyond where the slab surface would be. I finished the day with a call to Mark to see if he could help with the filling, or if he had any ideas. He promised to stop by "Early next week."

On Saturday morning I calculated how much insulation I needed for the foundation. I bought five gallons of asphalt foundation coating, sixteen sheets of blue foam board and a case of foam insulation adhesive in tubes. I was planning on taking Sunday off. My brother Ken was coming up for lunch and to check on our progress.

Sunday morning was clear, sunny and strangely cool. With such great weather, it'd be a shame to waste the few hours before Ken showed up. I put a metal cutting disc on my grinder and went around the foundation, cutting the forms wires off and chipping off the loose cement that had oozed out of the gaps in the forms. Still early, I opened the five gallon can of tar, put on rubber gloves and started to coat the outer foundation.

By the time Ken arrived the entire outside was coated up to grade. Time for a cold beer and a few guilt ridden hours off. My lighthouse project was now officially my lighthouse obsession.

Unlike retired folks, contractors start work early. When Mark had told me that he'd be by early in the week, I took that to mean Monday or Tuesday. He was at my door 7:30 on Monday morning. I jumped out of bed and pulled on my work clothes. This time we got to toe-kick on top of concrete walls.

It would take several truckloads of sand to fill outside and inside of the foundation. He said he could provide the sand and dump it at the beginning of the side road the excavator had used. But it wasn't clear how to get it to the site. I suggested that I could rent a bobcat and ferry it up the hill. A bobcat could move the sand, but they really aren't good for climbing hills. He said he had a John Deere tractor with four wheel drive and a 1/3 yard bucket, and a partner, Forrest, to drive it. We agreed that while I cut and glued the insulation boards for the inside of the foundation, he would truck in the sand and Forrest would run it up the hill with the tractor. Seeing they'd already be there with the tractor, I ordered a couple of loads of topsoil for future landscaping. There was no need face this same problem twice.

Delighted to have a solution to the problem of filling the foundation hole, I began to fret that I wouldn't have all the insulation in place by the time Forrest was ready to fill the inside. Yet another race. A couple of hours later, Mark had dumped the first ten wheeler of sand and Forrest was running the tractor up and down the hill. He back-filled outside the foundation as I glued insulation sheets to the inside. Good thing I'd coated the outer walls on Sunday morning. By the end of the day, as I finished up gluing foam insulation board to the last wall, Forrest was pouring sand into the foundation right behind me. On Tuesday morning we started the rest of the fill work early. As the sand piled in the hole, I pulled it down with a rake and hosed it down for compaction. By 6:30 that night the hole was filled, with an extra couple of bucket loads in the middle to compensate for the final compaction.

The foundation hole wasn't very deep. Spraying the sand with water made it firm to walk on, but to really compact it you need a machine. Forrest offered to lend me his gas powered compactor. The next morning he dropped it off and showed me how to use it. These guys were great!

The goal was to provide a nice, firmly packed sand base to support the concrete slab floor so it wouldn't settle and crack. I built a screed out of 2×4's, with guide boards on each end. This would set an even surface 3 ½" below the top of the foundation wall. I finished the compacting and still had time to swing by the plumber's office to find out when he could do the rough piping. The rough plumbing had to be in before I could schedule the slab to be poured. He thought he'd be available on Friday.

Friday came, the plumber didn't. I called and was assured that he'd be there on Monday.

Saturday and Sunday were too hot to work outside. I hid from the heat inside the house, tweaking my design plans and creating lists of materials to be delivered by stage for the rest of the project. If everything arrived at once it would be unmanageable.

On Monday I had to take a trip to Connecticut. After I arrived, I called home – still no plumber. I called his office. Another job didn't get finished in time and he forgot to call to reschedule. His guys were busy today.

Tuesday morning, I was home again. Still no plumber, but it rained most of the day anyway. That afternoon my friend, Larry, came down from Maine to visit and drop off some tools. He'd just finished building a porch and had no further need for his chop saw or Bostich framing nail gun. Not having to purchase these tools saved me a few hundred dollars, as well as the time it would take to buy them and get them delivered.

The next morning, another 7:30 knock at the door. By the time I got downstairs, the plumber was already in his truck and backing up to leave. I chased him down, brought him out to the site, and showed him the current plan for the foundation with the exact measurements of the shower drain, toilet drain and the hole for the septic pipe. After all the hassle getting him there, three hours later the piping was completed and he was gone.

Rough Plumbing

I called the building inspector to get approval on the pipes. Plumbing approved, I took pictures of the pipe layout for future reference, repacked the sand over the pipes and tamped it all down. I put foam insulation board over the top of the shower drain. The Styrofoam, one inch below the surface of the slab, makes future access to the pipes as simple as chipping out a thin layer of concrete. Hopefully someday someone does so, considering what it took to get those pipes done. I called Andy to tell him I was ready to have the slab poured.

It was now Thursday July 25th , and I was on hold until the slab got poured. I noticed a pool of water behind the uphill wall of the foundation. The soil was saturated and squishy. I dug a trench five feet from the wall to the downhill slope to prevent future problems. The water ran off and I laid the perforated pipe with a mesh fabric to keep the holes from plugging up. These unplanned tasks often delay schedules, but conveniently didn't in this case.

The report from the architect came. His recommended changes were for the most part simple. But, for some reason, he neglected to include the calculations with his report. Another unexpected hassle... Argh!

A Friday morning call resulted in answers to my questions about his recommendations and his promise to send a copy of the calculations. Thankfully none of his recommendations would be much more costly than time spent in updating the design.

The architect recommended that I sheath the walls with the first course of plywood mounted horizontally, the usual way. The next course should be vertical, overlapping the top of the first floor and the bottom of the second floor. Doing so would better tie the floors together and make the building stronger. The problem was that I now needed to redesign all four walls of the second floor so that the studs lined up with the studs on the first floor. Not having a CAD system, this meant a lot of redrawing. Not difficult, just tedious. I spent the better part of the weekend redesigning the stud positions and notating his changes on the plans. They included bolts every three feet around the perimeter of the second floor, in effect bolting the two floors together. I had already added the longer and more narrowly spaced anchor bolts to the foundation. With all the additional bolts and the plywood spanning between floors, for sure even in our high wind area this building would never blow down.

Waiting to get the slab poured, I kept busy fretting about building the walls. Walls framed with 2×8's are heavy. My concern was safely raising them without a strong assistant. After research on the web, I ordered a set of wall jacks that could more than handle the weight of the heaviest wall. Buying the right tools is a good investment. Even if you never use them again, you can always resell them.

Later that day I went to LaValley's with my first lumber order. It was big and would take a few days to fill and get delivered. I left instructions for the truck to drop it in front of the right-hand garage door.

My plan was to stack my materials in the garage in reverse order of use. Storing the lumber in the garage would protect it from the rain and, more importantly, the sun. Nothing can warp fresh lumber like a hot day in the broiling sun. As I needed stock, I'd pull it from the garage, cut it, and then hand carry it to the site. The closest point in front of the garage is also the place where the concrete truck would park while filling the wheelbarrows with cement for the slab. The wood couldn't be delivered until the cement truck left, and I still had no firm date on the slab pour. Monday was a possibility.

The cement crew arrived on Monday the 28th, and by 8:00 the cement truck was on site. Pouring the slab was slower work, because after filling wheelbarrows on the top of the wall, the crew had to push them down the path and over a couple of planks leaning against the foundation wall, before dumping out the concrete. The wheelbarrows wobbled as the planks sagged under their weight, but thankfully none fell over. By noon the cement was poured and the power-floated surface was nice and smooth.

Finished Slab

I checked on the order for the wood, and it would be delivered on Thursday. I'd use the interim to make some special tools.

A normal framing square wouldn't work with non-perpendicular walls, so I bought a large plastic one and cut an 11° piece from one edge using the radial saw. Then I made blocks with the same 11° angle for setting the tilt on the circular saw and bevel on the table saw. I would also need to mark and transfer angles onto wide pieces such as the

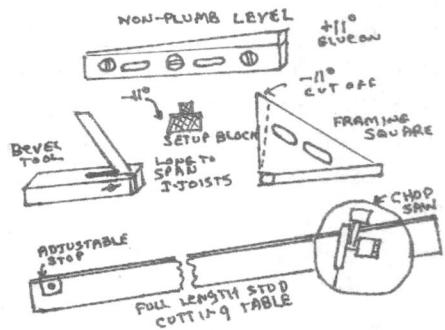

Special Tools to Build Slanted Walls

I-Joists. Using a block of wood and an eighth inch thick aluminum bar, I made a large adjustable bevel tool. It would also be tricky to check the slanted walls for plumb, so I attached a piece of 2×4 cut to the magic 11° angle to a level to do the job.

Every stud has to be cut on both ends to the same angle. I built an extension table for the chop saw out of 2×4's, with a stop block screwed to the table to avoid endless measuring and marking to get all the studs the same length. The stop block would easily adjust for the longer second floor studs.

I needed a place near the site and out of the weather to store my tools. The back roof of my garage has a three foot overhang to keep the firewood out of the weather. Beneath it I built a shelf to store tools on the end nearest the lighthouse. Below the shelf went the compressor. A couple of blue tarps were hung to keep out windblown rain.

It was now mid-summer, the last day of July. I had finally reached the point in my project where I wasn't waiting for any contractor. In the two months since first meeting with the building inspector, I'd worked with the dirt guys, the cement guys, the architect and the plumber. A foundation and slab are major accomplishments, but I had yet to put a stick of wood in place.

On Thursday morning, August 1st, I was up early, eager to drive a nail. But, unlike the dirt guy and the cement guys, the lumber truck guy didn't show up at the crack of dawn. The anticipation was killing me. At 10:30 they said the wood would arrive by 1:00. I needed to stay busy, so I fixed the lawn tractor. At 1:30 they said it would be there by 2:30. I decided to stop being a pest and switched my attention to cutting the long neglected grass. The lumber arrived at 5:00. By dark I had the whole delivery neatly stacked in the garage.

Chapter 9

Building the Wooden Parts

Friday morning my first real carpentry task was to bevel the outer edge of the pressure treated sills so the sheathing would sit flush. This is a messy job. Pressure treated wood is heavy and wet. You need to wear a mask. Whatever chemicals they used to keep the wood from rotting may have the opposite effect on your lungs.

I put a brand new carbide tipped rip blade into my table saw. Since all outside bevels are cut at the same angle, I used the special wooden block I made to set the blade for an 11° bevel. Using roller stands to support the wood, I muscled the 2×10's through the saw.

Positioning the sills takes careful measuring to make sure all the anchor bolt holes line up and that all four sides are equal in length with squared corners. By the end of the day all of the sill plates were seated on foam sill pads and bolted down. The wooden portion of my lighthouse was now officially just over 1.5" tall … only twenty-eight plus feet to go.

It was time to frame a wall. To reduce confusion, my assistant and I agreed on a naming convention. Side A faces east. It is the nearest to the garage and has a doorway on the first floor with a window above on the second floor. Going clockwise around the building, Side B faces south and has a window on the first floor but not the second. Side C faces the woods to the west. It has no window on the first floor, but one on the second floor directly opposite the Side A window. Opposing windows give an open feeling to the smaller second floor room and, supposedly, generate Feng Shui. As Side D faces uphill and a section of dense woods without views, this northern exposure has blank walls on both floors.

The first wall we tackled was Side B. We ripped a bevel into the outer edge of the wall footer, or bottom plate. The width of this plate is narrower than the sill because of the bevel down its outer edge. Its inner edge is square and lines up with the inner edge of the sill. The end of the plate also gets beveled. I drilled the holes for the anchor bolts, and made sure everything lined up. It is much easier to check the hole placement before the wall is assembled. I cut the top plate the same width as the bottom, but shorter because the tops of the walls are narrower than the bottoms.

Working from a stack of 2×8 studs, with their ends cut to compensate for the 11°, we laid out the studs between the top and bottom plates. The 2×8 studs line up with the outer bevels on the plates as they get nailed.

We left out the last stud on both ends because it wasn't clear yet exactly how they would tie in with the inward slant of the corner posts. On my two-dimensional plans the end stud and corner post intersect as they near the top. This intersection is sort of in a third dimension and figuring out the compound bevel for the studs is easier once the corners are in place. This may sound confusing. It is at first, but once you do one the others are easy. The corner posts don't go in until all four walls are up.

After assembling the Side B wall with its rough window opening, we added diagonal strapping to prevent racking. It was time to try out our new wall jacks. I built two poles using doubled up 2×4's. I cut safety straps from the metal bands that held the lumber together in shipping, and attached them to the bottom plate and sill. The straps would prevent the bottom of the wall from kicking out as the top was raised.

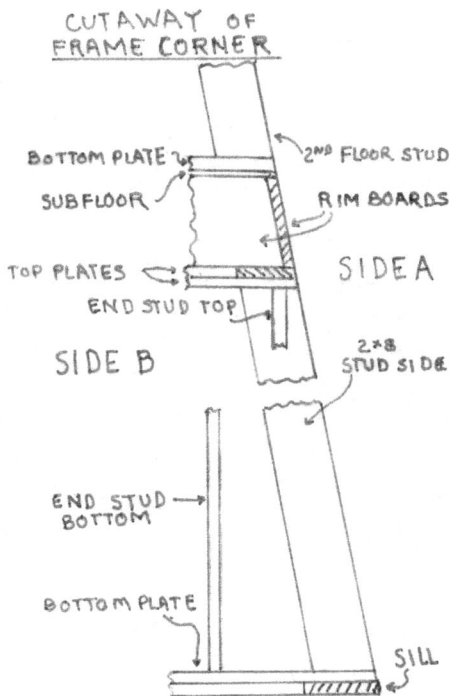

Side View of Framing

Jacking the First Wall

The wall jacks provide better safety and control than brute force when lifting the heavy wall. Standing on step ladders, we pumped our jacks in unison. The wall glided into place. When the anchor bolts protruded through the holes in the bottom plates, I cut the safety straps and the wall dropped over the bolts. After a quick check with my "un-plumb" level to make sure the wall was at the correct vertical angle, we added braces to temporarily hold it up. In just one weekend we'd mastered the arts of fabricating and raising a slanted wall. Probably no big deal for professional framers, but for us, a major accomplishment. We proudly took a picture of our now one-walled lighthouse.

First Wall Up

Monday, August 5th and we were eager to continue framing. The next wall to go up was Side D, directly opposite Side B. With no door or window, Side D was much simpler to frame. It went up without a hitch. These first two walls have longer top and bottom plates with beveled ends. They must stand at the correct angle so Sides A and C fit between them.

Side C, also a blank wall on the first floor, was next. This was a true test of our accuracy and planning. As we jacked it up, it slid snugly between the top and bottom plates of Sides B and D. Once verified to be at the magic angle, we screwed pieces of scrap plywood over the top of the corners to tie the three walls together.

We overdid it on Monday. Tuesday progressed slowly. I messed up the positioning of a couple of Side A studs when framing the door hole, and had to knock the wall apart and re-frame it. We didn't get the wall raised until late in the day. It too slid into its spot and got tied to the other walls. All four walls were up and it was beginning to look like a building.

Sometimes unexpected diversions can be entertaining. We'd been doing a lot of sawing on the slab and there was sawdust everywhere. After the water from one rain shower dried up, Mary Lou discovered the shape of a large fish had taken form in the sawdust. Maybe we weren't that far from the ocean after all.

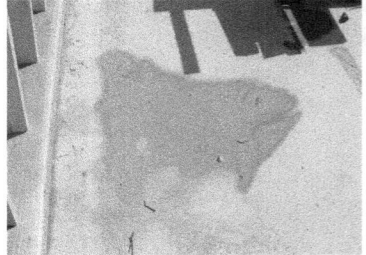

The corner posts were next. The architect recommended using solid 4×8 stock. Not knowing their precise length, I hadn't bought the them in advance. To get a rough length, I measured the distance between the bottom and the top plates at the corner and added a few inches for the top and bottom angles. After spending most of the next day going from lumberyards to sawmills, it became apparent that nobody in our area stocks 4×8 lumber. A special order could take up to "Two weeks... or so." Rather than use solid 4×8's, I'd make my corner posts out of doubled up 2×10's. This put more wood into each post and provided a greater contact area against the bottom and top wall plates. The larger doubled-up wood would actually be stronger than a solid post, considering knots and grain variation.

Before cutting the first post, I remeasured the exact gap between the outer edge of the bottom and top plates, and then cut the first corner post to length using my standard 11° angle. That didn't work. Although the corner posts and wall studs look like they slant in at the same angle, they don't. The corners lean farther into the building and are 14° off of square. I changed the angle and cut wood for a new post. I beveled the outer corners to provide a flat surface for attaching the sheathing. The two halves were then nailed together, slid into place, and nailed at the top and bottom. It would have been smart to bevel the inner edges for attaching the inside walls, but I hadn't thought about the interior finish yet.

Corner Post

With the walls up and corner posts in, the frame felt sturdy, but the last stud on each end of the wall adds even more strength. The inner side of each end stud needs to be cut away where the stud intersects with the corner post. The cut goes from zero at about one third of the way down the stud to over three inches deep at the top and is beveled to mate with the corner post. It took patience, a few pieces of scrap and several tries to get this crazy compound bevel right. A shallow angle rip is a deep cut. The mid-priced circular saw I'd just purchased smoked out after straining through two cuts. Cheap tools are no bargain. The more powerful Makita I replaced it with struggled a bit, but didn't burn out.

Thursday we cut the remaining three corner posts and nailed them in place. Then we replaced the plywood scraps that were holding the tops of the walls together, with 2×10 plates beveled on the outside edges. These plates tie the walls together at the tops, and form a solid base for the second story joists. Double checking the measurements showed everything was within a quarter inch of the plan... not bad for amateurs using dimensional lumber.

On Friday afternoon the truck arrived with the floor joists and rim joist material. The floor I-Joists have ½" plywood centers and

2 5/16" wide strand board flanges on the top and bottom. Though nearly 12" tall, they feel lighter than traditional lumber.

The rim joists attach to the ends of the floor joist similar to the way headers and footers work in a stud wall. With slanted walls, the rim joists need to be beveled on both edges and they get installed after the I-Joists. With the I-Joist height of nearly twelve inches, using dimensional lumber for the rim joists is not practical. It is better to use wider boards called rim board. These are made of glued up strands of wood and come as full 12×1¼ pieces 16' long.

Rim board is remarkably heavy. Though I'm sure they are water resistant, I still rushed to get them out of the rain and into the garage. Never rush when using power tools or moving heavy materials. I sustained my first job-related injury when the wet rim joist slipped from my hand and landed on my toe. I took Saturday off and watched the nail on my still throbbing big toe turn completely purple. I needed a day off anyway.

By Sunday I'd recovered enough to get back on the job. Making up the rest of the end studs for the first floor walls and nailing them in took most of the morning. I spent the rest of the day cutting nailing blocks with a bevel cut on their outer edges. They go between each stud at the height that the sheets of sheathing end. They make the stud wall more rigid and provide a surface for attaching the sheathing. This is tedious work, but sure uses up a lot of scrap.

Monday morning arrived and it was time to do some sheathing. Hanging 48 square foot sheets of plywood gives the perception of rapid progress. Holding up a sheet of plywood for the first course while nailing it in place is a two person job, and my assistant was on a mini-vacation in Boston. I screwed metal 2×4 hangers to the plywood and ran S-hooks through their nail holes. Using a pulley lashed to the top of the wall I was able to hold the plywood in place while nailing it.

My system worked well, and by the end of the day the first horizontal course of sheathing was up on all four walls. The second course would be mounted vertically per the architect's recommendation, and extend up the second floor walls. Since the second floor walls weren't up yet, this vertical course goes on later.

Chapter 10

The Second Story

On August 9ᵗʰ we began work on the second story. The floor joists and rim joists were too much for Mary Lou and I to handle. I called my brother Ken and told him I'd be ready in a couple of days to take advantage of his generous offer to help. Meanwhile, I cut the rim joists to the approximate length and beveled their top and bottom edges on the table saw. This allows the rim joists to have the same slant as the walls.

Ken and I set up pipe staging in the first floor to make it easier to reach and position the floor joists. We marked where the inside of the rim joists would be and measured for the full length floor joists. The ends of each full floor joist need to be cut at the magic angle to butt up against a rim joist. The rim joists for Side A and C go up after the floor joists are in place.

We ran our first floor joist from Side A to Side C and nailed it to the top of the walls. This joist sits about four feet from Side B and defines one side of the opening for the spiral staircase. We installed a piece of thick, heavy duty plywood four feet from the Side B and Side C corner. One end sits on the top of the Side B wall and the other end attaches to a hanger mounted to that first floor joist. This defines the second side of the stairwell opening. The dense plywood is engineered to support hangers for the ends of the shorter I-Joists that run from Side A to the stair opening. Once the staircase opening was defined, the rest of the joists go in quickly.

We were moving quickly and I wasn't wearing gloves. Hence my second injury. I was pushing an I-Joist up from outside the building and Ken was pulling from the inside when a splinter of strand from the top flange of the joist jammed under the pad of my left thumb. It went in deep and snapped off. I couldn't see it, but could feel it. By my estimate it was a half inch long and a quarter inch deep. It didn't hurt too bad, so I decided to wait a couple of days and see if it would work its way far enough out to get some tweezers on it.

By Friday we finished all of the floor and rim joists. The next morning I was eager to start laying the sub-floor. First I had to get the very heavy ¾" plywood sheets up onto the joists. I made a homemade crane, with a mast of doubled-up 2×4's, and a large eye bolt to hang the pulley. This rig helped get the decking up in short order.

The splinter in my thumb was still not visible. By the end of the day my thumb, more numb than sore, was turning a brighter shade of red. A trip to the emergency room seemed to be a good idea. After three and a half hours of waiting, and a half hour of slicing and picking, the splinter was out. It was as big as I'd thought, so the trip was worth it. The doctor said that it never would have worked its way out, and with proper bandaging and gloves I could continue with the project.

Rim Boards with Decking

On Sunday I shifted the deck plywood around on the joists and glued and nailed it down. I finished boxing in the opening for the spiral staircase on Sides B and C using the pieces left over from the ends of the rim boards.

The next day I cut the longer studs and beveled the edges of the headers and footers for the second floor walls. I laid out the frame for Side B, making sure the studs for the second floor lined up with the studs on the first floor.

With slanted walls, the higher you go the narrower the walls get. The horizontal width at the base of the second floor wall is enough shorter than the first floor to eliminate the need for those beveled end studs that take so long to fit.

On Tuesday morning we nailed up the studs and plates for Side B. The opening for the spiral staircase was a gaping hole in one corner of the deck. One step too many while focused on jacking up the almost 9' high stud walls, and I'd suddenly disappear down the hole. So I framed in a false floor over most of the opening, leaving just enough space to access the second floor by ladder.

It was time to raise the Side B wall frame. With the stair hole covered, I felt comfortable moving around one story off the ground on the 14' square deck. Space was a bit limited by the about-to-be-raised wall frame covering the majority of the deck. That's when Mary Lou rediscovered her fear of heights. She was fine standing at the center of the deck, but near the edge with nothing between her and the drop off was too much to handle. My reassurances of how safe it was didn't help. I was on my own.

After anchoring the foot of the wall frame to the deck with straps, I got to really appreciate the value of the wall jacks. I alternated pumps on each jack until the rising frame left space for the step ladders. Alternating between the step ladders, pumping each jack a couple of pumps per trip, I was able to do a single-handed wall raise. With no anchor bolts, it looked like the whole frame might go over the edge, but the straps did their job and the frame eased its way into place.

It felt safer laying out the Side D frame, having the Side B frame up behind us. It was really hot and late so we put off nailing it together until the next day.

I have a habit I call "fretting." Before I'm about to do something I haven't done before, and am not sure of, I fret. My fretting isn't simply worrying over doing something right. With me it's an involuntary act which can take over my head at any time.

Somehow it prefers doing so around three in the morning, taking the form of an endless thought loop. My mind repeatedly goes over all variables trying to anticipate any problems that might arise, and every possible solution. Fretting is tiring. I'd already used up countless hours of valuable sleep fretting the features of the design, working around the many steps of the concrete work, raising walls and cutting the compound angles on the end studs.

Although only one second floor wall frame was up, my subconscious mind must have declared victory over the second floor. That night it switched to fretting about building the lamp room on the top deck. The deck would be 12×12', slightly less work space than the second floor deck, but one story farther from the ground. Climbing up and down ladders all day carrying materials would be tiring, especially in the heat. I figured that building the lamp room wall panels on the ground might help. But, assembling them on the small deck would be difficult. Once the lamp room walls were up, the deck space for building the roof would be even tighter. Plus I'd have no assistant because of the height. Staging wouldn't help, because with slanted walls the higher up you go, the greater the space gets between the staging and the building. The biggest physical challenge would be cutting, fitting and attaching all of the rafters and shingles for the six-sided roof while working off an extension ladder.

The lamp room became a mental "show stopper." I even fantasized about buying a used bucket truck to whisk me and my materials up to the deck. The issues seemed endless, and I was spending hours every night building the lamp room in my head.

It was now August 18th and the hotter and more humid dog days were on us. The second floor Side D frame went up fairly quickly. With the two opposing wall frames erected, and no end walls, the building looked weird. But by the end of the day we almost had the Side C wall framed. Thursday and Friday felt like we were working in a steam bath. We were lucky to get one wall framed and two corner posts up each day before retreating to the shelter of the house. On Friday evening we stood back to admire our progress, and with the bones of all four walls of the second story up, the shape of the main building was now defined.

Taking Shape

The height of the building was now a real concern. Getting high enough to attach the plywood sheathing near the top required a long ladder. I was using an old aluminum 40' extension ladder split down into two separate sections. Each section was lighter to move, but with the lightness came increased flexibility. With my weight and the weight of the plywood, the ladder bent as I climbed it. My assistant insisted I put the two ladder sections back together for more stability. This fixed the flexibility problem, but doubled the weight and the number of times I'd move the ladder over the rest of the project. Had I fretted this problem, I'd have immediately bought a lighter fiberglass ladder. But in the back of my mind was the idea that I'd need that forty footer to reach the peak of the roof.

Finally, all that fretting over the lamp room paid off. One morning I awoke with a strategy. We would build the lamp room, complete with shingled roof, on the ground. Then I'd have a crane hoist the assembly over the garage and onto the deck. Why not? They'd already pumped tons of concrete over the garage. I had no idea what a crane cost, but was sure the cost would be justified by the work and time saved, not to mention the danger avoided. I could also take advantage of the flat driveway in front of the garage right where my stock got delivered, and save carrying all those materials around the garage to the lighthouse and up to the deck.

So many pluses and only one potential minus, the cost. I needed sleep, so the decision was made. Now all I needed to fret about was finding an affordable crane and operator that would be available as soon as the lamp room was ready to be moved.

The next three days were consumed with hanging plywood. We used up all of the plywood on hand. All of the vertical sheets for the second course were up, covering from the top of the horizontal sheets of the first floor to a couple of feet of the second floor. The third and final course would also be mounted vertically.

On Thursday I went to the building center to order the joists and plywood for the third floor deck. I also wanted to find out if they had a crane for hire. Good news, they did. Bad news, when I showed them a sketch of what I wanted to do, including how far the crane needed to reach, their crane was too small. Good news again, Todd knew of a guy who had a bigger crane. Even better, I knew him too. Andy, the guy who had done the concrete work also owned a crane that might just solve my problem.

A calendar milestone in New England is Labor Day. It marks the unofficial end of summer. Friday was the eve of the long Labor Day weekend, and that morning I waited for the delivery of my lumber, regretting that I hadn't placed the order sooner. Ken was planning to come up and help with the deck joists and floor. Without the lumber we'd have a long weekend off, something I couldn't afford. I reviewed my plans for the top deck. I double-checked everything, particularly the position of the lamp room walls relative to the hatch opening from the second floor.

By late that afternoon there was still no wood. I called the lumberyard. They told me it was on its way. An hour later I called again. They told me that it had already been delivered. I checked my driveway again. Maybe it had been delivered, but not here. I took a ride around the neighborhood and found that yes, my wood had been delivered, but to the wrong driveway. It was nearly five. We were going into a three day weekend and my material was nearly a half mile away. I made a desperate call to the lumberyard, which was about to close. They promised to make things right, and they did. An hour later a fork lift, carrying the errant materials, chugged up the driveway.

I spent Saturday cutting joists for the top deck. These were simpler, because the vertical fascia board ends are square, not beveled. Even though the span between walls was less than twelve feet, I used the same I-Joists as on the second floor. They'd provide more than enough support for the lamp room, which doesn't sit directly on top of the outer walls.

Hatch Opening and Deck Joists

Sunday... the first day of September. In my dreams, I would have had the building up by now. In reality, I had two floors up and partially sheathed.

Ken arrived about mid-morning and we nailed the rim joists and the first two floor joists in place. By Monday evening, after working through some scattered showers, we had the hatch opening framed and the remaining floor joists completed.

Ken was back on Tuesday morning. With him on the ground, hooking the line to the plywood, and me up top working the block and tackle, we easily moved up the sixty pound sheets of OSB plywood for the first layer of the deck. I shifted the sheets into place and nailed them down. Like Mary Lou, Ken has a problem with heights. Crawling around laying a deck that high up with no railings wasn't an option for him. I'm usually okay with heights, but even I felt a bit like a Flying Wallenda working without a net.

Next we hoisted the plywood for the second layer of deck and I got the full sheets nailed down. I handled the half-sheet pieces by myself after Ken left. The next day I had the second layer of the deck done. The building now had a flat roof and felt as tight as a fortress.

Thursday I snapped chalk lines for an equal overhang on all four sides, then I trimmed off the excess. I also put ½ inch plywood sheathing over the rim joists on two sides.

Friday after sheathing the other two rim joists, I was off to the lumberyard to pick up the 2×4 studs and plywood for the lamp room walls. The staging of all these lumber deliveries revolved around available space in the garage. Getting the materials under cover might sound like an unneeded precaution, but so far I hadn't had a single sun twisted piece of lumber.

Top deck on and without the lamp room, the building looked sort of like a Mayan pyramid.

Chapter 11

The Lamp Room

It was time to make our building look like a lighthouse. I set up saw horses in front of the garage door to cut and assemble the lamp room wall panels. By the end of the day we'd triple-checked our design and nailed the first panel together.

The lamp room has six walls. Five are identical with a solid bottom and a window opening on the top. We chose standard size, horizontal sliding windows because they look the most like lighthouse windows and can be opened for ventilation.

Framed Lamp Room Walls

Rather than a small door-like hatch for crawling out onto the deck, we'd opted to use a full size door. A standard prehung exterior door would fit nicely into the sixth wall panel, which is mostly a door hole. This saved the time it would take to fabricate a custom door frame and sill. The door window is similar in size to the sliding windows.

On Monday we assembled the six panels together in the driveway. Making sure that the angles all fit correctly takes a while. The driveway isn't paved, and the surface not perfectly level, so shimming was needed under the walls to get them all plumb. Even so, it was so much easier working on walls that didn't slant and walking around on flat ground rather than using ladders.

Tuesday the nice weather was replaced by rain. This provided an opportunity to review the design of the lamp room roof. Six-sided and peaked, it is similar to the roof of a gazebo. I'd originally found a roof design on the internet and scaled it to meet our lamp room dimensions.

Rafters run from each of the six corners to the peak. Shorter rafters run from the middle of each side to the peak. Finally, half rafters go on either side of the corner rafters to provide sixteen inch centers for nailing the roof sheathing... many pieces, lots of angles.

I'd thought of using 2×8's for the rafters, but 2×6's are more than sufficient for the size of the roof, even if loaded with snow. In a warmer climate 2×4's would probably suffice.

Center Pole With Rafters

Space is tight when trying to fit a dozen rafters into one spot. To simplify this, I made a short hexagonal vertical post using a couple of pieces of 2×4. Working from a step ladder, I nailed the post to a 2×4, spanning between the tops of two wall panels. The center of the post is at the center of the lamp room. This hexagonal post provides flat surfaces to attach the top end of each of the six corner rafters. Each rafter has a small triangular piece called a birds mouth removed from where the bottom of the rafter sits on the top wall plate. I worked out the final angles and position of the birds mouths with a little trial and error.

The middle rafters were trickier. The tops have to be beveled on both sides to fit between the tops of the corner rafters. These compound miters are difficult to envision and tougher to cut. Our first middle rafter also took some trial and error to get the correct fit at the top and birds mouth at the bottom. But after having done one...

With the corner and middle rafters in place, half rafters are fitted to both sides of each corner rafter. These too required compound beveling.

Six Sided Roof Rafters

Six-sided roofs are complicated. I hadn't taken a geometry class in over fifty years, and back then I only got a C. By the time all of these crazy cuts in the rafters were done I was ready to pull any remaining hair out of my head. Despite the heat and intermittent showers, by Saturday night the rafters were done.

On Sunday morning we rigged some pipe staging beside the lamp room and started sheathing the roof. With the roof overhanging at the eaves, the bottom edge of each roof segment is about 5' long. Using 4×8 plywood sheets would result in a lot of scrap. Instead, we used 1×8 ship lap boards and covered the whole roof with rolled ice dam material. The sheathing and waterproofing took two days.

On Tuesday we were already half way through September and just ready to shingle the roof. We'd selected a red asphalt shingle with a shake effect pattern that looked great in the brochure photos. Using standard shingles would have saved time, because they do not need to fit to a pattern. What should have taken a day took two, and the resulting shake effect is barely visible from the ground. That evening it looked like we would get the roof finished by Thursday night, so I called Andy to schedule the crane for Friday.

The next two days were a scramble. After completing the shingles on the roof I decided to fabricate a cap for the top of the peak out of sheet copper. With some custom fitting and soldering patience, the cap fit, dropped onto the roof peak and got screwed down. It looks like it was meant to be there.

Roof Interior

Shingled With Copper Cap

We pulled the protective tarp off the deck and attached some 2×4 blocks for positioning the lamp room as it was lowered onto the deck. The crane straps need a way to attach to the lamp room, so we built a boxed frame of 2×8's, and ran it through two opposing lamp room window holes. Any time left on Thursday afternoon was spent trying to close in as many eaves as possible. The showers didn't help. All but two eaves were done before we gave up for the day.

Though easier to install on the ground, we left the windows and the door out to save weight. I wasn't sure exactly how much the lamp room weighed, but with the roof shingled it looked heavier than the 700 to 800 pounds I had estimated when Andy calculated the crane's ability to pick up it up, extend it over the garage and lower it onto the deck. That night I fretted about needing a bigger crane.

Early Friday morning Andy and his brother showed up with the crane. It looked smaller than I'd imagined, and the distance to the lighthouse seemed farther.

They positioned the crane as close as possible to the front of the garage. The stabilizing pads were lowered and the boom extended. Straps were looped under the boxed frame and the crane slowly hoisted the lamp room into the air.

Lamp Room Over Garage

As it swung around and over the garage all I could think of was what I would tell my insurance company if it fell. "The top floor of a lighthouse fell through my garage roof." Luckily, the box frame was strong enough and the straps worked.

I rushed to the top of the lighthouse and climbed out on the deck, ready to guide the lamp room into place. In the distance I could hear the overload indicator beeping on the crane. They adjusted the angle of the boom. The beeping stopped. The lamp room hovered four inches above the deck. As they inched out more cable, I pulled the room over the locator blocks. It descended onto its spot. In less than an hour the most nail biting part of the project to date was over. The minimum cost of a three hour crane rental was well worth it. I was so stressed I took the rest of the morning off to recover. That afternoon I was back to work reviewing my plans for the window and door dormers.

The lamp room was up, but there was still a lot to do structurally. The four window and door dormers had to be framed and the deck roofed. Saturday I cut and assembled most of the first floor, Side B, window dormer. The opening in the wall looked huge

Dropped in Place

59

relative to the actual window size, but as the dormer frame came together the hole seemed much smaller.

Other than a trip to buy flashing, Sunday was a day off. By Monday I was back at it, working on the dormer from a stepladder. I didn't finish until Tuesday morning. We used the same shake-looking shingles as on the lamp room roof for the dormer roof. It took at least one trip up the ladder to fit each shingle to the pattern.

That evening I began calling around for a roofer to do the deck. I'd done my research on flat roofing and had decided to go with a rubber membrane roof. It looked as if I could do it myself, but I figured it was probably best done by a professional. The deck was narrow and high off the ground. It brought to mind an old Charlie Chaplin film about a wallpaper hanger. In my imagination, I saw myself perched at the top of a ladder trying to exactly position sheets of rubber covered with contact adhesive onto a roof also coated with adhesive. I enjoy working with wood, but flexible materials that instantly stick to each other on contact are beyond my temperament.

Dormer Roof on Bench

The next morning I had the sides of the Side C dormer up and was ready to frame its roof. This time I mocked up a sloped wall on my workbench, using scrap plywood and slanted at 11° off plumb. I cut, assembled and sheathed the roof frame. Then I cut, fit, and numbered each asphalt shingle.

The roof sub assembly was passed through the second floor window hole, set on the dormer sides, then lag bolted to the building. The flashing and shingles were added. By fitting each piece on the bench, I avoided endless trips up and down the ladder.

Thursday I used my bench assembly technique for the Side A, second floor window dormer.

That evening I met with the first roofer. The deck area to be roofed was small, as the entire deck is only 144 square feet. The lamp room covers 64 square feet, leaving approximately 80 square feet of actual surface to be covered. I figured a couple of hundred dollars worth for material and $10 to $15 per square foot for installation would be a reasonable price, including the 80 feet of flashing at the base of the lamp room walls and around the perimeter of the deck. The roofer looked it over, shook his head a lot and made comments about how this wasn't going to be easy and how he usually does much bigger jobs. He ignored my comments about it being a small job, all new construction and something he could probably knock off in a day or two. He said he wasn't prepared to give me an estimate. He thought the job should run about $3200, but only if he didn't run into any problems. And then added that he wasn't sure if he could get to it this year. I told him not to bother writing an estimate. No way was nearly $40 per square foot in my budget or would I agree to a deal with someone who can't offer at least a rough schedule. Maybe I'd have to reconsider doing it myself. But it was nearly October. Though the weather was still warm, temperature could be a problem, because the adhesive couldn't be used below freezing. I called a few more roofers, left messages on answering machines, then spent the next few days finishing the dormers for the window and the door on Side A.

Tuesday morning... yet another milestone... two months had passed since the first wood had arrived. The building was now at full height. With the dormers all built and with the lamp room on the top, the Mayan pyramid now looked like a lighthouse. No time for celebrating, though. We should have been weather tight by now and were still far from it.

Chapter 12

Getting Weather Tight

Being weather tight means sealing off any parts of the building that water, snow or ice can penetrate. Temperature swings during the winter can cause tremendous damage if water accumulates and freezes.

In a building with perpendicular walls, sealing the corners isn't a big deal. Most of the rain falls straight down and the rain that does get on the side of the building quickly runs down the wall. With slanted walls, rain falls onto every wall surface and it all runs down the side, increasing the risk of leakage. I used ice dam material that comes in narrow rolls to flash around the corners as well as where the top fascia meets the walls. With this material sunlight is an issue. It can start peeling off after a month or so of exposure to direct sun, and no way would we get the siding on within a month. I had to protect the ice dam and plywood sheathing. I decided to use felt paper, or what some people call tar paper.

That afternoon, I put in my order for the windows and doors. Windows and doors install quickly. Being stock sizes, I imagined they'd be readily available, and I had delayed in placing their order to avoid filling up my garage.

Wednesday, while eating breakfast, I watched the weather forecast. They were talking about up to 18 inches of snow in Montana and a hurricane heading for Louisiana, and then both possibly coming our way. In the past, we've had first snow here as early as mid-October and big snow in November. I ran the list of what had to be done through my head. I still needed to find a roofer for the rubber roof. I had to get the eight windows and two doors and install them. Then there was covering the entire outside with tar paper. I added a few other things like closing the two open eaves. What if that hurricane headed north, or worse, that blizzard headed east?

That afternoon I got through to another roofer. Without visiting the site, he was figuring about $3600, but not promising he'd meet the price or get the job done any time soon. Visions of buying a giant blue tarp and covering the entire building danced through my head. I went over to the lumberyard to see if they knew of another roofer, and to check on when the windows and doors would arrive. I got the name of a local roofer, but there was a backup in the window deliveries. The best date they could give was two weeks or so. Why, in a building recession, a window company would have a backlog of standard size windows just didn't make sense. The doors were in stock if I wanted to take them with me. This didn't help much. I couldn't put the lamp room door on until the deck roof was done and I didn't want to put the main door in until the window above it was in. I did pick up the doors, a couple of rolls of tar paper and a box of nails with the plastic discs on them. I could keep moving by covering the walls. As soon as I got home I put a call into the third roofer and started hanging tar paper.

That night the roofer stopped by on his way home from work. I showed him the building and told him what I needed done. He responded with the obligatory nods. I also told him what I expected the job to be worth. The good news, he assured me that his guys had done many rubber roofs and he'd do the job for about $1000. The not so good news, it would be one, two or three weeks before he could start. The rain had played havoc on his schedule and he had to finish his current job and another job ahead of mine. This was the best I could do, so I gave him the job hoping for dry weather and one, rather than three, weeks. Even though they were now forecasting that the two storms would miss us, the idea of that big blue tarp was starting to sound more like plan B than a crazy notion.

Thursday and most of Friday were spent hanging tar paper. This is a lousy job, particularly if working alone. The first sheet spans the whole wall across the bottom and wraps around to the other corner, covering the ice dam clad corners. Near the ground it isn't too hard to handle. Nailing in the ring nails with the discs on them is the pain. They don't like to go into plywood. When the hammer hits them they often bend or shoot out of your hand, which at the same time is trying to hold the paper level. I bought a stapler that works by pounding it against the wall, hoping to get in enough staples to hold the sheet up and then go back and put in the nails. "Whack it" staplers love to jam and are a pain to disassemble and clear.

Each sheet of tar paper overlaps the one below it to shed water. Once you get high enough to need a ladder, the job gets harder. Trying to hang a sheet while standing on a ladder and swinging the stapler is one step too many. If at least three staples aren't in and you let go of the paper, the staples rip through. The best way is to go right for the nails or grow a third hand. In hindsight I should have bought a used roofing nail gun.

Waiting for Windows

By Friday morning I had Side A and part of Side B papered. It started raining and I didn't want to put paper over wet wood. So I switched to nailing tarps over window openings. With the window hole above it on Side A now covered, I installed the entry door. I was sure the roofer and his crew were taking the afternoon off too.

That night the weatherman talked about a new big storm, this one was in Wyoming and almost sure to come our way. New Hampshire weathermen, eyes bulging and voices excited, seem nearly orgasmic when making panic forecasts about the season's first snow.

Saturday began dry enough to finish papering Side C and hang a few sheets on Side D. When the rain came I switched to inside work. The engineer had recommended bolting the sole plates of the second floor through the top plates of the first floor, using 3/8" bolts spaced at a maximum of 36" apart and starting no more than 12" from each corner. Just the job for a cold and rainy day. I made up bolts long enough to span the distance between the plates using threaded rod, nuts and washers.

On Monday it was dry enough to hang tar paper again. By Thursday evening the weather talk was of how the blizzard we didn't get was now somewhere in Canada. All of the tar paper was up. It may have looked like a tar paper shack, but it was closed up, even if only with tarps over the dormer windows, the lamp room windows and the top door opening.

On Friday the windows arrived and I got the first one installed on Side B. As eager as I was to install the rest of the windows, I couldn't. My son, his wife and her parents came up to spend the weekend. His in-laws were visiting from China, and although they seemed impressed by my workshop, it wasn't clear they had any idea why I was doing what I was doing. Not being fluent in Mandarin, I couldn't tell them my story on building a lighthouse in the woods. Her dad took lots of pictures. They probably returned to China with stories of insanity running in our family and the photos to prove it.

Monday brought more rain... a good opportunity to get rid of the scrap pile. We moved two pickup loads of scrap end pieces, plywood and assorted trash to the dump. It seems offensive paying to buy materials and then paying again by the pound to get rid of the scraps. But the site was much neater without the scrap pile. Now if it snowed we wouldn't have to wait until after the spring thaw to clean it up.

Tuesday the weather broke and I made a ton of progress. The windows for Sides A and C on the second floor went in without a hitch. I moved up to the lamp room and put in the five slider windows. With no railings on the deck, I felt safer after looping a rope around myself and the lamp room to keep me from inadvertently stepping back to admire my progress.

Windows and a Door

Wednesday the roofer called. He was planning to start Thursday afternoon. The forecast was for rain that night. The deck was currently dry. To keep it so, I nailed tarps to the walls of the lamp room and draped them over the sides of the building. To prevent them from blowing in the wind I walked the ladder around the building, nailing the bottom of the tarps every couple of feet.

Then I went to the lumberyard for wood to trim out the doors and windows. It is more convenient to just call and have the wood delivered, but with trim boards, getting them yourself gives the opportunity to pick over the stock and avoid getting the pieces the last guys picked over and rejected.

I used 5/4" pine to trim around the triangle outline on the dormer sides and between them 1" pine. The difference in thicknesses accentuates the shape of the sides.

Thursday I trimmed around the main door and cut the pieces for one of the window dormers. The roofer called. The forecast was rain. We agreed it best to wait until Friday.

Dormer Trim

Friday the roofer and his crew arrived to do the flashing and lay the rubber roof. It only took a few minutes to rip off the tarps that took so much time and effort to hang. While he and his three helpers maneuvered around each other on the 80 square feet of open roof, I trimmed out the Side B window dormer. By the end of the day, the rubber was down. It looked great, except for the bubbles. He told me they'd probably go down as the cement cured. Then he put some plywood pieces on top of the membrane, explaining they should press the bubbles out overnight.

Saturday morning the plywood was lifted off. Bad news. The bubbles hadn't disappeared, they had grown larger. The roofer made some phone calls. It appeared that the glue might not be compatible with the OSB plywood I'd used for the deck. Theoretically the interaction of the glue and the OSB generated gas that got trapped under the rubber. He assured me that he'd fix the problem at no extra charge, and since the flashing was up, if I put the lamp room door in it wouldn't be in his way. He left, promising to come back as soon as the right glue was available.

Mary Lou had already put primer on the lamp room door. Now I had to get it up to the deck. Hanging over the deck and pulling it up by rope didn't look like the safest option for me or the door, so I opened the hatch opening to the lamp room to full size. After removing the door from its casing, I hoisted the parts up through the hatchway. The door frame just barely squeezed through. I reassembled the door and casing, and it slid neatly into the wall opening. Once the knob was installed, the door closed tightly. The only exterior lock sets available locally had built in locks. Dreading the possibility of someone (me) accidentally getting locked out on the deck, I used an interior lock set without a lock. If it doesn't weather well it is cheap enough to replace.

The lamp room was weather tight except for the last eave boards, which I hadn't had time to make up before the crane had arrived. I planned to wait on doing these until I had railings up, but the railings couldn't go up until the bubbles were fixed.

Sunday, October 20th was a chilly morning. At least it hadn't snowed yet. I continued trimming out the dormers. Each piece of trim was custom fit and tacked into place, then removed and taken down for painting.

Mary Lou primed and painted them in the warmth of the house. After I finished cutting the trim for one dormer, she'd paint the pieces while I cut out the next one. Our process was efficient, but finish work is time consuming. We plugged away on the trim for the rest of the week.

Still no verdict on the bubbles under the membrane, another one of those aggravating problems that are impossible to anticipate. By Friday night the end was in sight for the trim work. We took the weekend off to visit our grandson on his first birthday.

On Monday we were back on the job, refreshed by not looking at the lighthouse for two whole days. It was time to have the framing and sheathing inspected. I called to schedule the inspector only to learn that he had retired and we had a new building inspector. Even though the plan had been approved and everything built far above any building code, it wasn't reassuring that someone unfamiliar with the project and seeing it for the first time would have final approval.

Trim work was nearly completed by Tuesday night. It was October 29th and the weather was definitely New England late autumn. By now lots of people were discussing the bubbles. The glue maker claimed the roofer did something wrong. The roofer blamed the glue. The weather was still barely warm enough to apply new glue. My biggest concern was if the roof didn't get fixed before things froze, I wouldn't be able to put up the railings on the deck or those last two boards to close the open eaves.

That afternoon two solutions were proposed. The first was to leave plywood laying on the rubber for thirty more days in hopes that the bubbles go away. The second was to remove the rubber and try again, closely following the guidance of the glue manufacturer, and supposedly a different glue. I didn't believe some disappearing bubble miracle would occur. The rubber is nonporous, where could they go? In thirty days it would be far too cold to glue down a new roof. I took a stand and insisted the roofer replace the membrane.

Wednesday I awoke to the first snow flurries of the year. While waiting for the building inspector to arrive I went over the railing plans. I wanted a design that met code while allowing maximum wind flow through the railings. This would reduce the potential for snow getting trapped and piling up in the space between the railings and lamp room. One alternative was the least lighthouse-looking but probably easiest. The perimeter of the deck would have 4×4" cedar posts at each corner and midway down each side. Between the posts would be 2×4" cedar headers and footers, with stainless steel wires running horizontally four inches apart. This would allow maximum air flow. The other plan was the same except instead of wires I'd substitute 3/8" stainless rods set vertically on four inch centers. These were more costly, but would look better than the wires.

That afternoon not only did the new building inspector arrive, the former inspector came with him. I was relieved to have the guy who had originally approved of the design there. They signed off the building. We discussed the two railing alternatives and they made a good point about how kids love to climb, and someday some kid might get up on the deck and try climbing the horizontal wires. I decided to go with the vertical stainless rods.

Thursday I went to the lumberyard and picked up cedar for the posts, headers and footers. I also ordered some anchoring brackets on Amazon. I don't like railings that anchor to the sides of the rim joists because they never feel really tight. The brackets I ordered bolt down through the deck, creating a socket for the post.

Friday November 1st ... the weather is definitely colder and still no new roof. I went to a metal yard and bought a bunch of 12' stainless rods. Once home, I began the long tedious process of cutting the rods to size using a reciprocal saw with a "Flame Thrower" blade. Working with steel in the cold is far less enjoyable than working with wood, and stainless steel is hell on saw blades.

On Saturday morning it warmed a bit. The roofer and a couple of his guys showed up with new glue and rubber membrane. He assured me that this time there would be no bubbles. While they stripped the old roof off I went back to cutting rods.

By the end of the day, the new roof was done, no bubbles and no added charge for the rework. I also had all the rods cut. It took another whole day to cut the cedar headers and footers, drill the holes and press the rods into them using long clamps. The post anchors had arrived, fittingly via the post office.

Mary Lou painted all of the cedar. I spray painted the outsides of the 2×4 hangers for mounting the horizontal railing sections to the posts and the caps for the top of the posts. I carefully measured the deck, marking exactly where the posts would go. With a closed loop rail system there is little tolerance for error.

Thursday morning I mounted the anchors to the cedar posts. Each anchor is made up of two L shaped steel brackets. Each bracket attaches to two sides of the post and has two flanges for bolting to the deck. Bolts through the post connect the two brackets. Wood screws attach the brackets firmly to the post. It sounds like a good design, but the bends for the flanges weren't precise. The result was the posts didn't necessarily have all four flanges flat on the deck. If a flange is not sitting flat on the roof, the post will either tilt or not touch the deck on all sides. I cut a bunch of shims in the shape of the flange base from ice dam material. They would go beneath any flange that didn't touch the roof to ensure a plumb post and water tight seal.

Drilling Holes for Post Anchors

Saturday morning we began putting the posts up. I used 2×4's cut to five feet to ensure proper spacing between them. I was working off the ladder and Mary Lou was assisting, sitting on the deck. After all of the trouble in getting the rubber roof down it seemed crazy to drill 32 holes through it. We reviewed each measurement at least twice before drilling the four holes per post anchor.

Nylon shoulder washers went into each flange hole and lag bolts went through the deck into 2×6" blocks, which we had glued to the bottom side of the decking inside the building. That afternoon all of the posts were up and plumb. We hoisted the fence-like horizontal sections up through the inside of the building. They dropped into the hangers on the posts and were secured using long sheet metal screws. The railings brought the final definition to the structure.

All that was left to make the building weather tight was to close the last two eaves. Then we needed to run the electricity out to the building, put in stairs, insulation... The list was long, but we would keep plugging at it until the weather stopped us.

Sunday I moved the table saw, the radial saw and a workbench out to the now nearly weather tight building.

Our plan from the start was for cedar shingle siding. Though I wouldn't be putting up any shingles until spring, we needed to decide on how we'd do the corners. There were two alternatives for the corner trim. The first was a Boston Weave where there are no corner boards and the end shingles overlap each other, alternating on each course. This produces a nice looking corner, but was the time required to do such fancy work worth the look? I only had enough pipe staging to shingle one wall at a time and couldn't go round and round the building to overlap the corners. The other alternative was corner boards, or what some people call rake boards, where pine boards run up each side and overlap each other. We went with this much simpler approach, which is also less susceptible to damage than the softer cedar.

On Monday morning while Mary Lou was off attending a Veterans Day event, I measured and cut corner boards. One side of each corner was a 1 ¾" wide piece, and the other was 2 ½", giving a 2 ½" face on each side of the corner. Each board got beveled top and bottom to avoid water running down the butt joints. They also were cut so that the butt joint on one side of the corner didn't line up with the one on the other side. All the pieces got tacked up to make sure they fit, then removed for painting.

I then started laying out and cutting the final pieces of trim for the fronts of the dormers. The most difficult place to trim is the center triangle of the dormer on Side A, a second floor window. Reaching that spot is difficult with the lower doorway dormer in the way. The triangles are trimmed using 5×4" stock. Between the trim boards I used tongue and groove bead board. I used the same materials to side the lamp room below the windows, giving the look of a wheel house on a wooden ship.

Wednesday was too cold to work outside. Just the thought of climbing an aluminum ladder gave me shivers. I was back at it Thursday morning. By Saturday night all of the dormer trim and eave boards were cut, painted and nailed in place.

Sunday was spent cleaning up the site and organizing what lumber I had left. It was time to think staircase. My plan had been to pick up a used spiral staircase on Craig's List. They're usually inexpensive secondhand because a lot of people who put in spiral staircases wind up switching them out.

I measured the staircase height and reviewed a copy of the latest building codes for spiral staircases. With the higher than normal first floor ceiling, nothing available would fit. I'd wait a few days to check for new listings. More listings got posted, but none the right size, and though some listings were for nice older cast iron units, none met current codes.

We decided to bite the bullet and buy a built-to-order spiral staircase. It would comply with all current codes and fit the lighthouse exactly. Several online companies looked good. We went with Mylen Stairs in New York. After several phone calls and our approval of their design, I placed the order. Shipment would be in four to six weeks. The new staircase cost more than I wanted to spend, but was one less thing to fret about at night.

My focus switched to wiring, the code for grounding, and figuring out the needed materials. The main panel in our house is in a utility room that shares a wall with the garage. First I measured how much cable it would take to get from the utility room, through the wall, and around the inside perimeter of the garage to where the cable goes through the garage wall and into conduit to the lighthouse. A special flat cable was needed on the section from the garage to the lighthouse because with underground conduit the wire needs to be waterproof. The top of the conduit going down the exterior wall of the garage has a sliding section to accommodate for frost heaving.

Tuesday I priced out the materials at an electrical supply house and a "box store." The electrical supply house was surprisingly less expensive, plus they had people manning the counter who knew all about wiring, even to the point of recommending odds and ends that I hadn't anticipated. Armed with rolls of cable, junction boxes, a sub-panel and various breakers, I had enough to keep me busy for days. After mounting the sub-panel in the lighthouse and running the flat cable underground and through conduit, I drilled a through hole into the garage. The next day Ken came up and we routed cable around the garage into the utility room. By that night all of the connections were complete, and I had power to the lighthouse and even a utility box mounted for plugging in my saws.

For an unattached building, the sub-panel needs its own earth ground. The ground is an eight foot long copper coated steel rod that is driven into the ground. A heavy gauge wire running through conduit connects the ground rod to the sub-panel. This is a simple job if the rod goes all the way in before hitting ledge. While excavating the foundation hole we'd hit ledge at around five feet on the deep end. In ledge areas it is supposedly acceptable to lay the earth ground on its side as far down as it can go. Some people say, if that is the case, there should be more than one earth ground. Either way, digging another trench was not an appealing solution. I figured I'd try my luck a few feet farther from the building than where the excavator had dug. Using a two pound hammer I started driving the rod down only to hit ledge at around four feet. I pulled up the rod and tried again a couple of feet away and got lucky. I must have found a crack, or a place where the ledge dropped off, because I got the entire eight feet into the ground.

Sunday November 24th, happy sixty-eighth birthday to me. I took the day off. I was back to work on Monday. I bought the number 6 wire to connect to the rod, laid some conduit a few inches deep and completed the grounding. The weather was getting really cold and my back was starting to complain. Nearly four months from the day that the first lumber had arrived, I declared an end to my building marathon for the year. Though not shingled, the lighthouse was built and weather tight. From now on we would work at a slower pace on interior projects. It would no longer be an everyday project... at least until the spring.

Winter Arrives

Chapter 13

Finish Work

As much as it was a relief not having to cram as much as I could into nearly every day to get the building closed up, I missed getting out there and working on it. There were many inside jobs to do over the upcoming winter, just at a slower pace. I bought a tank-top heater, a thirty pound propane tank and a monoxide detector. With them I could heat the yet-to-be insulated building without fear of asphyxiating myself with monoxide.

I bought a pile of electrical boxes, outlets and wire to keep me occupied any time I had the desire to keep the project moving. Being a workshop, the plan was for outlets every three feet. Extra outlets are cheap, but involve more labor when putting up the inner walls because the slant of the walls makes mounting receptacles trickier. If the outlet boxes are mounted flush with the sloped walls the receptacles face downward. There are two ways to avoid this. The first is to frame in short vertical knee walls. That would make it easy to have the receptacles perpendicular, but waste precious floor space. The second, which I chose, is to mount the boxes to the studs with a tilt. This makes the receptacle plumb, but creates a new problem in attaching the face plates… discussed later.

It was now December. Even without insulation, the space heater kept me from freezing on most days. I finally got to use my workshop as a workshop and built my grandson a maple toy chest for Christmas.

Around the end of the first week of December, the weathermen were spouting off about "Dipping down jet streams" and the "Polar Vortex." I'd never heard about Vortexes before, but it sure was cold. The day that the first plow-able snow arrived, so did the staircase. I got a call mid-morning on December 10th from a trucking company. The staircase was in the truck and just one town away. The driver was calling to make sure there was enough room for him to turn around in my driveway. You'd think a company that delivers bulky items would ask that question before putting five hundred pounds of staircase components into a forty foot long semi. Our driveway is 800 feet long with about a 30 foot wide pad in front of the house. Even on a warm summer day you couldn't turn a tractor trailer around on it.

Fortunately, I had a pickup truck. We agreed to meet at a parking lot downtown and transfer the ice cold metal staircase parts from their truck to mine. I then toted them from my driveway through the snow to the lighthouse. Everything was stowed safely indoors just after dark.

After New Years I cleaned up the mess from my toy chest project and enlisted Ken's help to assemble the staircase.

The staircase looked sturdier than I'd expected, but the railing gave me pause. It was plastic tubing with molly screws to attach it to the balusters. Initially it seemed shoddy to me, but in the end turned out fine.

I started by nailing horizontal 2×4 supports in the corner of the hole where the two sides of the top landing attach. These

Staircase Installed

would act as a shelf to help support the landing while positioning the center pole. We put the pole where we thought it should end up and lowered the top landing over it. With the top positioned and pole plumb, we marked its final position on the floor. We removed the landing to lower the individual steps down the pole, then replaced the landing and screwed it to the sides of the hole. The landing held the pole up, leaving just enough room for a ladder so I could get back down from the second floor without having to climb out a window.

The stairs were positioned and anchored to the pole using set screws. Each baluster has to be to cut to length with a hacksaw before the railing is attached. The whole job took about a day. Later I drilled holes into the slab and used wedge anchors to bolt the base plate to the building.

Round Stairway in a Square Hole

The stairs were now functional, but a round staircase going through a square floor opening doesn't look very good. I needed to make the hole round. Many of these finishing steps were above and beyond the original plan, but this is where a little extra effort can make the building look much better.

I nailed pieces of 2×10 to the three corners that needed to be rounded and stapled sheets of poster board to them. The fourth corner remains square because of the landing. Using a string, a pencil and the pole as a compass, I drew the curve onto the poster board. After trimming the excess cardboard, I had a set of templates. I cut curves into scrap 2×8's to match the templates, and when nailed in place the corners became round. Pieces of plywood decking with matching curves tie in the floor. I finished the sides with ¼" inch thick decorative tongue and groove beaded pine cut into about 14" pieces. These 5" wide flat strips are flat, but look curved when nailed to the circular frame. A couple of ¼" thick by about 1 ½" wide strips of clear pine bent to trim the bottom and top edges give a finished look to the now round hole.

Rounding the Hole

Beaded Trim

With the rounded opening for the staircase, a straight railing around the top wouldn't do. I couldn't find a curved railing that would match the job, so I made one. Using a compact metal bender, some flat ¼" by 1" steel, and a lot of patience, I was able to make matching top and bottom pieces for a curved railing. I cut the balusters from the same ¾" square steel tubing as on the staircase. A trip to Maine to visit my friend Larry, who has a TIG welder, and the railing took on its final shape, matching the curve of the stair hole.

Round Railing

The next project was to build a stairway from the second floor to the lamp room. I fretted over several designs. One involved a ladder that could be moved on a garage door track and rollers to the wall. This would leave more floor space when not in use. I was fascinated with the idea, but the couple of square feet gained by rolling the staircase didn't justify constructing the custom roller system. A folding ladder like those used to access attics would take no floor space when not in use, but they look rickety, and getting one to both fit the opening in the ceiling and long enough to reach the floor would be difficult. I decided to build a stair ladder deep and strong enough to feel like a staircase. An added plus was it would leave enough space above for thick Styrofoam panels to insulate the hatchway in the cold weather.

The side rails of the ladder are 5/4×8" pine with a dado for each stair tread. The treads are 5/4" pine about 8 ¾" wide. I rounded the front edges and added beading in the top surface of the treads with a molding bit. The fourteen steps mount into the dado cuts in the rails. We did the finish work and assembly in the warmth of the house. The rails were painted white and the treads left natural with a few coats of varnish. After screwing it all together and plugging the screw heads, we had a very sturdy and good looking stair ladder.

Stair Components

The handrails for the stair ladder have to be strong enough to be pulled on and simple enough to build. I was fretting their design when I came across a TV show called "The Haven" on Netflix. Shot in Nova Scotia, it has some great interior lighthouse scenes. One of them showed a stair ladder similar to the one I'd built. It had a railing system made up of black iron pipes and fittings. I used ¾" pipe for the hand grips and ½" pipe for the stanchions.

They connect using standard tee fittings, ell fittings and mounting flanges. The box store even cut the pipes and threaded the ends to size for free. After cutting the overhangs from the round flanges and adding a coat of black enamel, the railings were done. Problem solved for about $90.

The pipe railings work well until you near the top of the stairs. Then you need something more to hold on to for the last few steps into the lamp room. I used a length of 1" braided rope to span the gap beyond the end of the pipe railings. It is knotted through eyed lag bolts on the lamp room floor and part way up the frame next to the door.

Pipe and Rope Railing

Time to finish the electrical. I wired in outlets, switches, ceiling light fixtures and smoke detectors. The first floor ceiling light and the light above the stairwell are on dual switches. The lamp room got outlets and a dual switch for the lamp, with one end in the lamp room and the other just inside the main door. I didn't do any outside work other than one cold trip up a metal ladder around the end of February to reattach a sheet of tar paper the wind had knocked loose.

Part way through March the weather started to break and I was eager to start shingling. I bought a siding nail gun and stainless ringed shingle nails online. I ordered white cedar shingles from the lumberyard. Our plan was to stain the shingles. White cedar takes stain better than red. I also bought four shingling guides, a neat tool to mount the ledger boards. They are easily adjustable and slide up under the last row of shingles. This eliminates the need to puncture the showing surface of the shingles with nails.

I watched videos of how to stain shingles. It looked easy. You make up a tub, fill it with stain and simply dunk the shingles. The excess stain drips off and voila, shingles stained on all sides. Apparently there was nothing to it. We wanted our lighthouse white, so I bought a couple of five gallon buckets of Cabot white stain. It's an opaque white coating much like paint. However, unlike the thinner penetrating stain I'd seen in the videos, the excess does not drip off. The stain penetrates, but a lot of it clings to the surface.

We went to Plan B, using a roller. We set up a work space in the garage and strung ropes between two ladders. The roller put on a smooth coat without drips, and the wet shingles were hung with clothes pins on the lines to dry.

While Mary Lou rolled what looked to be a million shingles, I prepared the building by cleaning up some torn tar paper. Then I replaced the plastic washer ring nails with roofing nails, as the washers stick up enough to keep the shingles from sitting flat. I finished putting up the last of the corner boards and snapped

Shingle Staining

chalk lines all around the building to make sure that the first two shingle courses lined up with a five inch reveal.

Using a radial saw I cut a bunch of shingles to various widths, having the magic angle on one edge to fit up against the corner boards. It was time to start hanging shingles. I began on Side D, a good wall to learn on since it has no windows. As I finished the first course, I realized I should have decided on how I would heat the building because it would be easier to drill, make exit blocks and flash the access holes for the propane feed and heater exhaust before shingling. I researched heaters online and decided a medium size

Shingles and Corner Boards

Rinnai would do the job. New propane heaters are expensive. Craig's List had a reasonably priced secondhand Rinnai 456 that seemed more than adequate to heat our little building. I had our propane supplier check the heater out. We determined where the holes for the gas feed and exhaust pipe would go through the wall. I put blocks with perpendicular faces and flashing in those spots and scheduled for him to run the gas line and hook up the heater.

The shingles were now going up faster than they could be stained. I set up pipe staging as I worked my way up the wall. As we neared the top, the building slope became an issue. Even with my long arms it was a stretch to reach the wall, so I bought a set of staging outriggers to get closer to the building. On Sides D and A the ground doesn't fall off, and working on the outriggers felt safe. By the time I got around to Sides B and C, where the land fell away behind me, it felt a lot more precarious. I ran a rope around the building to keep the staging in place and bought a roofers safety harness to keep me in place.

Last Side Shingled

Before nailing the final course of shingles, I put up the top fascia trim boards and flashing. The roofer had used drip edge to flash around the edges of the deck which left the ends of the first ply of decking exposed. I made up edge moldings to cover them by cutting off one side of the U-shaped plastic covers designed to protect the top of deck joists. They slip up under the edge of the drip edge and under the bottom of the decking.

The fascia trim boards are very wide due to the height of the floor joists. Rather than wide boards that might buckle, we used two narrower pieces of ship lap pine. They overlapped each other and the rabbet on the bottom edge overhangs the top course of shingles. Before stripping the staging we decided to give the shingles one more coat of stain. Hot weather, cedar shingles and applying thick stain with a brush made for slow progress and seemed to use a huge quantity of stain.

Yet another plan B situation. I masked off the painted fascia boards, end boards and dormer trim. We switched to an airless power painter. Starting at the top, it took longer to strip the staging as we went down than to apply the stain. The savings in stain and time on just one wall more than paid for the sprayer.

By mid-August the shingles were all up and everything was white. The weather began to cool enough to take on landscaping. The excavator had left the start of a rough stone wall about ten feet from the foundation across Side B. This needed to be added to and built up. We also needed a wall on Side C, but the flat ground on Side A and D didn't require a wall. I wanted the look of an island with the rip rap effect of broken granite. The local gravel pit turned out to be the ideal source.

They blast out granite ledges to make chunks of granite to crush into gravel. Many of the blasted pieces are small enough for one person to carry, and the flat ones make great cap stones. The best part was the price, about $15 for a pickup load. You have to load it yourself, but you also get to pick the stones. Seven loads, a lot of sweat, and a couple of weeks of work resulted in two dry fit walls. I back filled them with the topsoil we'd brought in when we filled the foundation.

Stone Wall

All that was missing was a front doorstep. This was one of those situations when you ask yourself why you hadn't done it sooner, like maybe before climbing up into the doorway hundreds of times? A local granite quarry cut an 18×10×60" step for about $150. It took a couple of hours with a long crow bar to muscle this weighty stone from my pickup bed and set it in place. A bag of grass seed and the landscaping was finished by mid-October.

Next on the list was insulation. Foam insulation sprayed between the studs and under the top deck seemed the way to go. In a couple of days everything is done, without having to deal with fiberglass. The only foam guy I could find took over a week to show up. He looked over the building and told me that he might be able to get to it in a month or so. I asked how much. He said he couldn't be sure but would do detailed measurements and he'd send me a written estimate in a couple of weeks. Another case of someone who doesn't want to be there when you find out what the cost will be. Rather than wait two weeks, I pushed for a budgeting, won't-hold-you-to-it price. He said "I don't know, maybe around seven." I realize that it doesn't take much skill or time to spray foam and the material itself couldn't be too expensive, but $700 for both floors and the top ceiling didn't sound right. He agreed. He was talking in thousands.

I bought fiberglass bats, rubber gloves and a respirator for less than a thousand dollars. Unlike on those old TV ads, installing spun glass insulation is not a fun way to spend a weekend. It's lousy work, but I was done insulating in less time than it would've taken to receive the foam guy's outrageous estimate.

For Christmas I built my grandson a maple bookshelf in my now heated and insulated lighthouse.

We took the whole winter off. Other than ceilings and wall board, flooring upstairs and a ton of interior trim, the building was more finished than most lighthouses I'd seen. At this point we could have declared a victory and simply used it as a workshop. But having gone so far, why not make the interior look as good as the exterior?

By April I was ready to do some decorating. The easiest solution would be to drywall the ceilings and walls. Drywall is cheap, comes in big sheets and goes up quickly. But we wanted an old look that drywall couldn't give.

First we needed to pick the type of ceiling. We decided on pressed metal ceiling tiles, a "tin ceiling." The two foot square steel tiles are available in a wide variety of patterns. We chose tiles embossed with a five by five pattern of stars. The joists have to be strapped at one foot centers, and hanging the tiles, which have dimples stamped into their edges to help orient them, isn't difficult.

The room size didn't lend itself to an even number of tiles, so I centered the star patterns and used a pebble grained pattern around the border. I cut the tiles at the edges of the stairwell to match the curve. I trimmed the edges where the metal ceiling meets the stairwell wood with plastic edge molding. A series of slots cut into one face of the molding made the molding flexible enough to follow the curvature of the opening.

Tin Ceiling and Vent

88

We weren't putting a heater upstairs at this time, so I added an air register through the ceiling in the opposite corner from the stairwell in hope of creating a convection loop.

Now for the walls. The tin ceiling gave the old feel that we were seeking for the room. We decided wooden walls would go well with it. Match board might work, but vertical planking on the sloped walls is more difficult, and the narrow boards might introduce too many lines into the room. Instead we went with 1×8" ship lap mounted horizontally, with the smooth surface out to avoid catching the flying saw dust from my power tools.

I fitted nailing strips ripped to 45° up each corner post to anchor the ends of the planks. The outlet boxes were mounted perpendicular to the floor. I made up a router jig to cut tilted openings into the pine so the covers would mount flush on the boxes.

Finishing the insides of the door and window dormers was time consuming. The sides we insulated with foam board covered by MDF fiberboard.

The upstairs floor we made of knotty pine planks screwed down and bunged with maple dowels. Oil based varnish gave the flooring a honey colored finish and turned the bungs dark brown.

Second Floor Ceiling

For the second floor ceiling we used narrow bead board painted sky blue, like a porch ceiling. After strapping the ceiling we ran the beading from Side B to D so the lines would fit better with the room and the hatchway to the lamp room.

On the walls we used ship lap again, this time rough surface out. Around the hatchway opening I used the same trim as on the spiral staircase. I cut blue insulation board left over from insulating the

89

foundation into a two piece block. It can be slid up under the hatch to prevent heat loss during the winter.

We painted the first floor walls a light gray with a slightly darker gray trim. On the second floor we used the same light gray for the trim and did the walls in white. Though primed with knot sealing paint, the knots still bled through giving an antique look.

Pine Floor and Railing Cap

I made a pine cap for the second floor railing using pieces of scrap pine cut to follow the curve in the metal. Gluing and screwing together two plies made a 1 ½" thick banister cap which when varnished matched the floor.

It was finally done. After three summers and part of one winter the building was done.

Everything looked right, except the lamp room light. From the beginning I had planned to use an airport runway light with a plastic Fresnel lens that my nephew had found at a yard sale. I had mounted it on a platform hung from the center of the cross bar in the lamp room. For a lamp, I'd bought the highest powered light available from a company in Pennsylvania that makes backyard-lighthouse beacons. It came with a glass domed housing, like the bubble gum machine lights on the top of a "Smokey and the Bandit" cop car. It looked cheesy, but you couldn't see it inside the runway light housing. What I did like was its mechanical drive that steps the motor down to about six rpm.

The runway light housing was too wide, and got bumped every time I opened the door to the deck, so I took it down. The domed light still worked without the Fresnel lens, but was now visible.

One morning while driving through town, I found the solution to this problem. Hanging in the window of a secondhand store was an old ship's anchor light with a thick crystal glass Fresnel lens. The antique copper lantern, made in Scotland in the 1880's, stands 18" from base to the chimney top, and is 9 ½" wide.

The Lamp

Originally an oil lamp, it had been electrified decades ago. I stripped out the old wiring. After careful measurement I discarded the original metal base that came with the dome light. I replaced that with a smaller base plate of non-conducting phenolic plastic to which I mounted the A/C motor and light. The smaller base fit up inside the Fresnel lens. The result looks quite nautical hanging in the middle of the lamp room, and throws off a decent beacon. We measured the lamp altitude. It's 1345' above sea level, probably making ours the highest lighthouse in New Hampshire.

The lamp room will remain an unfinished space. With the hatch closed it is a comfy, private space ideal for writing or just looking out over the surrounding mountains.

We recently watched a U. K. home buying show in which the Realtor asked the buyer to define what rural meant to him. The buyer replied "A lighthouse on the top of a hill in the middle of nowhere." It's reassuring to know I'm not the only one who thinks of such things.

91

Conclusion

This project took a lot longer than we ever would have thought. If I hadn't kept a daily journal of what we did in the first year, looking back on it would be a blur.

Some things that I hadn't worried about when going into the project had the greatest impact to our progress. The biggest was weather. I had always thought of our central New Hampshire summer climate, for the most part, to be moderate. It may be a global weather phenomenon or maybe in the past I never paid much attention, but during the first season when we were doing the bulk of the outside work, there seemed to have been an unusual number of hot, steamy and rainy days. I'm sure the weather slowed us down.

Another was the site work. My primary goal and focus while planning was the wooden part of the building. I didn't appreciate how much work and time is involved in site planning, digging and cement work... all of which have to be completed before the first stick of lumber gets cut. I should have begun those activities much earlier when the weather was cooler.

A third is the complexity. I knew going into the project that building a lighthouse was not a serial event. Particularly in the beginning, the project was a juggling act to coordinate the architectural work, the excavation and cement work, and the planning, trying to make sure one didn't get in the way of another.

Some things I fretted turned out better than I had feared. In the past, when we were building the house, we lived about a hundred miles away and had some bad experiences with local contractors. Maybe living at the site made a difference, or maybe we were just luckier on this project, because for the most part the work with contractors went smoothly. Everyone seemed willing to accommodate our schedule and delivered on what they promised. In some cases they gave a lot of valuable guidance and more help than expected.

Being a do-it-yourself type, I naturally approached the project thinking I'd do everything myself. My wife and brother had volunteered to assist, but I didn't think I'd need them very much.

Mary Lou knew little about construction and had never done that kind of work. We also found out early in the project that she had a fear of heights. By the end of the project she was as good as any carpenter with a nail gun, and comfortable sitting with her feet hanging over the edge of the deck to help with the railings. Ken, though better acquainted with construction, is also height averse and even older than I am. He gladly showed up whenever I needed him, putting in many hard days of work. I had underestimated how much help, both physical as well as emotional, they both would be.

I greatly appreciate the thoughtfulness shown by others. Magdalene, Mary Lou's cousin, painted the "Newport Light" sign for over the door. My son gave us buoys for Christmas, and Pat and Ken gave us a wind chime with the tones of the Bar Harbor light.

Perhaps my biggest concern had been my own ability to physically complete the job. My mental attitude has always been "I can do anything." But what you think you can do doesn't always match what you really can do, particularly considering the time it takes to do it. I don't think of myself as old, but after a few hours digging, or working off a ladder on a hot humid day, I sure felt it. Quite a few days ended earlier than I would have wanted. Fortunately none of my moving parts broke down and I actually felt more physically fit at the end of project than I did at the beginning.

As much as I struggled to prevent project creep, once we got the structure up we were so pleased with how it came out that we put a lot more into finishing it than planned. It became far more than a workshop.

Asked if I would do it again... definitely yes. Asked if I *could* do it again... I don't know. I might be better off just enjoying my workshop. I hoped you've enjoyed reading my story as much as I have enjoyed telling it.

Views from the Top

Visit our website www.ibuiltalighthouse.com for more photos of the project.

www.ingramcontent.com/pod-product-compliance
Lightning Source LLC
LaVergne TN
LVHW021540080426
835509LV00019B/2744